You are a tremendously talented hard working professional with superior talents who would be a valued service provider to many companies – if only you could gain access to companies who can afford to pay you what you are worth.

This book summarizes and relates actual step-by-step methods and winning scripts that get the meeting with the top level decision maker.

$1,000,000 sales <u>are</u> possible with these strategies.

See page 5

"Scott, your coaching program has been very helpful to my sales team. Everybody met their goal this month and one person was able to triple the number of appointments set after exposure to your strategies. The recorded teleseminars you did with my group and later sent to us on CD reinforced all the ideas and strategies you shared with us. Thank you."

Al Estrada

"I bought your book after hearing you speak and quickly was able to improve my appointment setting ratio. Your tips on dealing with prospects as groups and not individuals, how to make maximum use of prospecting time, and **how to deal with objections, put offs and send me information excuses have really made a difference.** Now I need some tips from you on improving my closing ratio. When is that book going to be released?"

Paul Jarosik

"I liked the format of the presentation – getting a simple outline. I liked the actual outline or steps of the call process. Over the years I've never had a structure of the exact steps – what you do next makes it easy to get through without floundering."

Kathy Bossi

"Enjoyed your prospecting tips and scripts. They will come in handy to grab our prospects' attn."

Andrew Carlson

"Right to the point, very informative."

Brian Edwards

"Dynamo! Scott speaks authoritatively and motivates effectively. He related marketing concepts directly to my practice in ways I can use. I'm all fired up."

John O'Brien

"Excellent ideas for getting to decision makers and setting up work station."

Midian Evans

"Very good techniques on getting in the door. Liked the alternative methods of handling a call, letter, etc. Creating a list that mirrors your best clients is an excellent idea."

Hal Billerbeck

"This program opened my eyes to different approaches, I never would have thought of. Its also interesting to hear solutions to problems that I, myself have failed at".

Eric J. Davis

"The steps toward the objective are segregated into distinct, concise, do-able steps that are not so overwhelming. Speaker has perfected the approach by doing it himself. Great job. Thanks."

Mike Semones

"Scott is the first resource employed by my firm that brought true value and meaning to the sales training sessions. Although I have been selling technology products and services for over 10 years, he was able to bring a fresh, clear approach to prospecting for leads and developing relationships with prospective buyers."

Cyd Tomack

"1. Liked how to sell an appointment with a top decision maker over the phone 2. How to get by receptionist/secretary and directly to the boss."

Edward D. Hines

"I liked the step by step procedures to getting a meeting. I also liked your input on contact managers."

Gary O'Connell

"Excellent ideas on use of fax and letter to gain contact after phone fails. Scripts are a great idea for ensuring you get the goal of the call accomplished."

James R. Andrews

"Scott is upbeat and his points are concise and relevant. His awareness of the needs of a sales person is excellent. Scott has a great approach to appointment setting".

Kevin Giroux

What I liked…"The goal setting and maintaining a prospect pipeline. New ways to get info from the gate keeper. Using voicemail to my advantage".

Jim Merriam

A personal note from Scott..

A quick $1,000,000 sale from a cold call sales appointment is not possible...right.

On the opposite page is the note from the VP of sales on a copy of the service agreement for a $1,000,000 new account closed on the 2nd meeting from a cold call appointment I set with a very senior executive at a $3 billion dollar company.

This client was a smaller player in a highly competitive industry dominated by a few gorillas. Their sales team could close deals when they were able to present to top decision-makers.

Prior to yours truly, four different consultants had been brought in to help them gain access to top executives with more than 1,000 employees. Those four attempts failed.

The first year implementing the strategies related in this book generated 500+ meetings. This $1,000,000 contract is just one example of the many major accounts that were closed as a result of those meeting.

What might these strategies do for your business?

Service Agreement between ~~Kawasaki Bros Co and ABC~~

This agreement is entered into by and between ~~Kawasaki Bros Co~~ (hereafter ~~Kawasaki~~ Bros.) and ~~_____~~

~~____~~ agrees to arrange the following services related to the shipment of household goods and personal effects for transferees designated by ~~Kawasaki Bros~~ including: counseling, packing, pickup, transportation, delivery, unpacking, claims settlement, and auditing.

~~____~~ will work with each transferee to coordinate scheduling with designated carriers and related contractors, issue necessary orders for, expedite, trace shipments, and facilitate the proper performance of services by all transportation carriers and related contractors.

~~____~~ will arrange the storage of household goods and personal effects for transferees designated by ~~Kawasaki Bros~~ and will negotiate all storage and insurance terms in the best interest of the ~~Kawasaki Bros~~ and transferee.

~~____~~ will audit all vendor service invoices for accuracy and compliance with ~~Kawasaki Bros~~ relocation policies, procedures, and authorizations, and will invoice ~~Kawasaki Bros~~ within 45 days of the delivery of the shipment.

~~____~~ will provide full replacement cost protection up to $50,000 to ~~Kawasaki Bros~~ at a cost of $155 per shipment. Additional coverage may be purchased through ~~ABC~~ at a rate of $.40 per $100.00 of declared value.

~~____~~ guarantees 180 days of Storage-In-Transit at the full discounted rate before shipments convert to Permanent Storage on all interstate moves.

~~____~~ will provide comprehensive SmartReports on all ~~Kawasaki Bros~~ transportation activity on a quarterly basis.

In exchange for the provision of these services for an estimated annual volume of approximately 200 domestic moves, ~~Kawasaki Bros~~ agrees to pay ~~ABC~~ service invoices which will reflect the following cost components:

- a ____% discount on all charges off of current rates excepting valuation and third party charges.
- a ____% discount on storage-in-transit and related charges
- a ____% insurance related surcharge (IRR)
- a ____ 75 per move Service Fee on all intrastate, international and self-haul moves

accepted for ~~Kawasaki Bros Co~~

Cindy ~~_____~~

date: 12/19/94

accepted for ~~ABC~~

~~_____~~

date: 1/9/95

Handwritten annotations across page: "Start / $1,000,000 / This is not possible / Bravo!"

With this book you will learn...

- How to select the pool of targets most likely to provide the sales results you seek.

- How to identify the real decision-maker.

- How to organize yourself for efficiency to make the most calls.

- How to generate conversations with decision-makers.

- What to say after you hear "hello" which maximizes the chance that they will conclude that it is worth 30, 45 or 60 minutes of their time to meet with you.

- How to respond effectively to resistance.

- How to convert conversations to appointments.

- Why it is important to think in terms of groups.

- How to provide targets a way to enter your sales pipeline without speaking to you.

- How to obtain value from the unreachable and those who say "no."

- How to sort and prioritize targets to properly allocate scarce resources of time and money for follow-up.

- How to efficiently and easily follow-up consistently.

How you will benefit financially from consistently being able to set sales appointments with top level executives at targeted high profit potential prospect companies.

1   You avoid sales peaks and valleys.

2   You don't miss out on opportunities that are out there anymore.

3   You gain control over your sales life.

4   You gain value from those who are unreachable or have no immediate need.

5   Prospects will start to call you.

6   Your prospects will be warm.

7   More accounts, revenue, profits and higher margins.

8   Your closing ratio improves.

9   You can easily follow-up for future sales.

Setting
Sales
Appointments

How to gain access
to top decision makers
at your most desired future
accounts (and your
competition's best clients)

Scott Channell

NEW MARK PRESS

Published by New Mark Press.

ISBN: 0-9765241-0-4

First printing: November 2004
Second printing: June 2006
Third printing. December 2007

All brand names and product names used in this book are trademarks, registered trademarks, or trade names of their respective holders.

This publication is designed to provide accurate and authoritative information with regard to the subject matter covered. It is sold with the understanding that the publisher is not engaged in rendering legal, accounting, or other professional advice. If legal advice or other expert assistance is required, the services of a qualified professional person should be sought.
—— From a *Declaration of Principles* jointly adopted by a Committee of the American Bar Association and a Committee of Publishers and Associations.

Contents

Acknowledgements

I owe a great debt to the many clients who, over the past 13 years, gave me the opportunity to learn and refine the process in this book.

In particular I would like to thank Michael Thames, Sean Shea, Lucy Pastore McCarthy and Denis Lavallee. Working with these superior VP's of sales taught me much about selling. Also, Bob Murphy, a consummate sales professional whose example had a major impact on my sales thinking.

Thank you to my wonderful daughters, Joanna and Kelly, for bringing me constant joy which makes projects like this possible. To Karl and Debbie Wilson for 34 years of friendship, support and encouragement. Special gratitude is owed to special advisors, role models and sounding boards namely Bob Butler, Bert Waters, Julie Bartkus, Joe Perry, Sue Dahl and Chris Jaeger.

My appreciation also goes to Gail Lowe and Ellyn Bogdan-Olsen for their assistance and judgment.

SCOTT CHANNELL

Is available for speaking, training, and coaching engagements.
Request a full catalog of services and products.
39 Dodge St. #288, Beverly, MA 01915
Phone (978) 927-5099 ● Fax (978) 964-0199
www.settingsalesappointments.com
scottc@findingbusiness.com

This book is dedicated to my parents,
Arthur and Winifred Channell

Special recognition and thanks to...

John F. Brotchie Jr.

Who could have guessed when I walked into a small local advertising agency 24 years ago that I would meet a man with marketing savvy, creativity and copywriting ability that has not been matched by anyone.

John makes every marketing and writing project he touches rise to a higher level. This book was no exception. His editorial assistance and guidance made the near impossible happen.

I am so fortunate to have his help.

1

How You Benefit From Access

Meeting more of the right people face-to-face in quantity will improve your closing ratio and bank balance remarkably.

Let me guess. You are a sales manager, salesperson, business owner or entrepreneur who has a quality product or service to sell, and you say to yourself "If only I could get in front of the right person, the top decision maker, on a consistent basis, I could make a lot of sales, make a lot of money and do some good along the way."

Well, in your hand are proven tips, strategies, techniques, shortcuts, organizational tools, scripts, fax forms, measuring devices, call patterns and follow up methods that you need to start scheduling face-to-face sales appointments with targeted top level "impossible" to reach decision makers - within days.

The goal is to provide you with step-by-step guidance to gain access to top decision makers at high value prospect companies.

You and your team will learn to do this repeatedly, consistently and without drudgery.

NO MORE TORTURE

One of the challenges to being successful at identifying great new business opportunities is to overcome the feeling that you are torturing yourself while you are prospecting. People aren't in, nobody returns voicemail. People don't get back to you, it's hard to talk to the real decision makers. People won't make a decision, they waste your time. You know the drill.

The process outlined in this book will substantially eliminate the torture element from prospecting. Torture is eliminated because people don't seem to mind investing time when they believe that their efforts lead directly to superior sales results... and commissions.

If you are an individual salesperson, there is no reason why you can't have your basic system up and running and be setting desired sales appointments within two weeks.

If you are a sales manager and you are getting a team running, the wheels tend to turn a little slower and it might take a month to get your system established for your whole group. But the steps, the process and the strategies are the same.

2,000 SALES APPOINTMENTS – REAL EXPERIENCE

In the course of my prospecting career I have personally set more than 2,000 appointments with top level, typically VP, Executive VP, CEO, President level executives of larger corporations.

These are the people who are impossible to reach. They are never in. They have layers of protection. Yet you will learn techniques in the next few hours that have consistently gained access and new accounts worth millions of dollars.

This process has worked with many varieties of consulting and service businesses and industries as diverse as relocation, energy management, high-tech, transportation, manufacturing, media sales and graphic design.

All of these industries are "different." Yet the means by which you can gain access to those who can sign checks are substantially the same.

The strategies I am going to relate to you are all born from actual experience. On the job, smiling and dialing, following up, faxing and conversing... and with all the scars to prove it. Prospecting is tough work. Most people hate it. I don't think I ever met anybody who loves to prospect. But I can tell you that when you are disciplined enough to follow a system that works.... results always follow.

Quality leads, conversations with decision makers, appointments with decision makers, appointments with decision makers at the right time to make the sale, flow from consistently following a system that works.

I have made and seen all the mistakes that can be made and they will be laid out for you in this material so that you can recognize and avoid them.

Setting sales appointments with top level decision makers is not rocket science. There isn't one thing you will hear that will wow and amaze you.

You will learn all the little tips and strategies that make you most effective and efficient at each and every step of the prospecting process.

Understand and appreciate this. Your personal prospecting system and results will only be as good as your weakest component. By that I mean you might be great organizationally, but if you lack the discipline to make the calls. You won't get good results.

Maybe you make a lot of calls but you stink at selecting the right targets, so a lot of people you speak to are low worth, low probability prospects and little happens.

Maybe you are organized, make a lot of calls but are not adept at getting targets to pick up the phone. You'll be frustrated quickly.

If you get a lot of targets to pick up the phone but your opening script is poor, you won't get results.

If you engage targets in conversation, yet are poor at responding to resistance, you will lose many meeting opportunities.

If you don't know how to generate significant value from the unreachables and those who say "no," a lot of prospecting time will be wasted.

Maybe you are good at everything but follow up. You are going to leave a lot of money on the table.

You need to be able to identify all the steps of a successful setting sales appointments initiative and be good at every step. If something isn't working, you need to know what to fix.

THIS IS NOT A COOKIE CUTTER SYSTEM

There is no one system best for every situation. But I believe this wholeheartedly. The components of successful prospecting systems are the same. The difference is how you decide to allocate your time and resources and how you define an acceptable result.

Some examples. Somebody just starting out or trying to get a new business off the ground may be willing to visit any prospect anytime. A more established business might choose to meet only with prospects that meet specific criteria such as type of engagement, credit worthiness, volume or profit margin may be a bit more selective about who they choose to go out and see.

In both circumstances the system and the process is the same. What is different is how they put different levels of emphasis on different components of the prospecting system to deliver the results they seek. You can learn how to make these adjustments to meet your various sales needs.

Everything that you will learn has been tested and proven in the real world. I am an expert on these matters simply because I have made every single mistake you can make when prospecting. Not only that, in order to make sure I had it right, and my mistakes were really mistakes, I went out and made many of them over and over again just to be sure.

Collectively all these little strategies and slight edges and organizational methods add up to create what I think of as a prospecting engine, an engine which, when you keep it running will generate qualified leads and quality sales appointments for you at the best time to make the sale for a long time to come.

2

Benefit Financially By Appointment Setting

Ten specific ways quality appointments improve your budgeting, cash flow and profit margin.

Let us review all the benefits that come to us when we are effective and efficient prospectors. We are, by the way, only effective and efficient when we can consistently and cost-effectively set sales appointments with the person who can authorize checks at those companies that are clones of our best and most profitable clients.

1. YOU AVOID PEAKS AND VALLEYS

How many times have you have had this problem? You are either too busy to handle all the business you have, or you are dying for dollars desperate to generate some sales and cash just to stay afloat.

When you are in that boom or bust cycle, you know that something very bad is happening, which has long term negative consequences for your business.

When you're dying for dollars you take business you should not take; you make price concessions you shouldn't make; and you make promises for delivery and quality that are unrealistic. This sets up expectations in your prospect's mind that are certain to be dashed. And this, of course, guarantees dissatisfied clients, more client churn and lower profits.

Many times what also happens when you're in a rush to book business is that you short circuit your internal procedures and practices. To book the business, you shortcut your production or service processes. Before you know it, you have no processes, just chaos. This quickly leads to business decline and failure.

To avoid these peaks and valleys, you're going to learn to always deal from strength. You won't have to cut your profit margin on projects, because you'll know with confidence that you're going to have a steady stream of qualified prospects coming up who are likely to buy at full price.

2. YOU WON'T MISS OUT ON OPPORTUNITIES
ANY LONGER

The good clients are just waiting for your call.

A sad, unfortunate fact for anybody in business is that there are usually a good number of accounts who would be very happy to do business with you... who would appreciate your service and pay a fair price. But they are denied the opportunity to benefit from your services simply because they are not informed.

They don't know about you. They don't know the benefits you deliver or how credible you are. They don't know what you can do for them. It is only that lack of knowledge that is denying them the opportunity to benefit from your services.

Why are they denied? Why don't they know about you and the benefits you deliver?

Simple! You don't identify them. You don't get their attention. You aren't there at the right time. You don't touch them.

They, therefore, lose the opportunity to work with you... a great service provider and you lose a great client who would pay well and provide a steady stream of profits for you over a long period of time.

You will not lose out on these opportunities anymore. You are about to learn how to identify all the potentially good quality clients within your service area, and you're going to learn how to identify the top decision-makers within these prospect companies and work through them methodically.

You will learn to use specific benefit-laden words with surgical precision. These carefully selected words will concisely summarize your value, slap your prospects to attention and overcome their resistance. If they have a potential need for your services, they will "raise their hand" and identify themselves to you. If they don't need you right now, you'll know how to properly evaluate them so that you can decide how and when to follow up — or not.

Most of the projects I have worked on involved major sales, big ticket items or services selling for $250,000 or more. They typically involved a 3 – 18 month sales cycle and multiple decision makers. After a couple of projects, I realized that most of the time we reach people when they *don't* need us.

I also came to realize that there is an untapped well of revenue and profit potential among the no's and unreachables.

Why are so many of these potentially very profitable accounts never going to write a check to you? Probably it's because your system doesn't enable you to follow up efficiently and effectively. The process you use probably doesn't allow you to identify and differentiate the mega-type opportunities from the average or low-profit or no-profit opportunities. If you don't know the difference, your limited resources will be squandered.

As you will soon learn…even when you can't reach your decision-maker, your calling effort can lay a foundation for significant future opportunities.

3. YOU ARE ABLE TO CROSS THE PROSPECTING CHASM

There are a lot of tricks and gimmicks "out there in the field" that people tell me work.

Can you build a business around gimmicks and tricks? Can you sustain growth around gimmicks and tricks? Not usually.

In the same breath people are telling me they know about some prospecting tactic that works, they tell me they don't practice it.

You need a system that is sustainable day in and day out; week in and week out.

When you implement this system, here's what happens every single time. In about six weeks, you will have booked a ton of good solid appointments. But you'll also create a problem.

Not only do you have to prospect for appointments, you have to show up. And then, because they are good worthwhile appointments with qualified people who can afford your product or service, you are going to end up going back 2, 3 or 4 times in order to close a substantial size deal.

And once you book the business, of course, you have to service it.

So it always happens. You will shortly have to cross the "Prospecting Chasm" where you have to Prospect, Sell and Service accounts. If you are one person, it is extremely tough for you to do all 3 functions superbly.

You have to be very focused and ruthless about weeding out the "no's" and the "maybe's." You also have to be very good with time management. You may have to delegate substantially most (if not all) of your appointment setting functions to a lower level person who can perform those tasks adequately. You may not believe this person can prospect as well as you... they don't have to. They only have to prospect adequately.

You'll have to consider that as an option down the road. If you set up a system that generates plenty of opportunities for your pipeline, but only you can set the appointments, your whole prospecting system will collapse. You're just not going to have enough time to prospect, sell and service. Prepare for this.

4. YOU GAIN CONTROL OVER YOUR SALES LIFE

Perhaps the greatest benefit of being able to consistently set sales appointments with top decision makers at companies that have an ability to pay full value for your services... is that you are in charge of your sales life.

You are in charge. Not your prospects. Not your clients. You.

When somebody wants you to take 10% off or they threaten to go to a lower priced competitor, you'll tell them to take that deal and you won't care.

When somebody asks you for impossible delivery times or tells you that they have expectations that just are not realistic, you'll walk from that prospect.... and you won't care.

You'll drop all those small accounts that are a pain in your neck... all those low-margin or no-margin accounts that you currently service just to get the business... and you won't care.

You see, when you know (*really* know) and have confidence that new leads and inquiries will continue to come on schedule as a result of your system, you're going to be far more selective about who you do business with. You'll know from experience that a certain percentage of those leads, inquiries and appointments will convert to new accounts. You'll know how long it will take and what the average size and profit margin of those new accounts will be. You'll have a base of experience from which you can intelligently allocate your time to gain the highest return. You will have the confidence to say "no" to business that isn't what you want.

As you develop a steady stream of inquiries and appointments. You will learn quickly which are most likely to convert to profitable accounts. You can make a conscious decision as to where to allocate your time for best results.

Maybe there will be a certain segment of your market which contains longer term, larger revenue more prestigious type accounts. You will have these prospects identified and you will decide how much time to devote to them.

There may be another class of account consisting mainly of your mid-range, bread and butter type clients that can be counted on for decent profit and revenue on a regular basis. You will decide how much time to spend on those accounts.

You may have yet another class of business account that sucks every bit of mental energy and motivation out of your business because you constantly have to listen to complaints, whines and impossible demands while working for mini-money or no profits at all. You will learn to identify, avoid and discard these blood suckers.

5. YOU GAIN VALUE FROM THOSE WHO ARE UNREACHABLE OR HAVE NO IMMEDIATE NEED

You will also benefit from perhaps the most powerful weapon in your prospecting arsenal. I call it "Plan B."

What do you do with the majority of people who you cannot initially reach? What do you do with the majority of people who you do reach, yet don't immediately agree to see you? Are those calls wasted? Far from it.

When I started setting appointments with high-level decision makers thirteen years ago, the game was simple. Call targeted organizations. Identify the top decision-maker and get them on the phone. Then slay them with a powerful 30-second script. They either agreed to a meeting or they didn't. That was it.

There were very simple short-term economics that had to be met. I had to book enough appointments that would convert within a reasonable time to an acceptable average sale so that the prospecting efforts would justify the time and money invested.

But, over a period of time, as I tracked what was happening, I realized that in a big-ticket sales environment most people I tried to contact were unreachable. Most people I did speak with said "No." Yet, I also realized that many of those people, at some time, would have a need and be prime candidates for the services or products my client had to offer.

Your "Plan B" will enable you to leverage the information gathered during your calling efforts so that tremendous future value can be reaped.

6. PROSPECTS WILL START TO CALL _YOU_

You get leads. People will call you to inquire about your services. With very little additional work (and very little expense I might add), this system is going to enable you to easily and cost-effectively manage a communication system that will have prospects calling *you* when they have a need.

7. YOUR PROSPECTS WILL BE WARM

When people are touched by us consistently over a period of time, they become better educated about the benefits we can provide them. When they hear a consistent message over that period of time, we create a perception of credibility in their eyes. So, by using this system, you will more easily interact with your prospects. When you do call them, meet with them or respond to their inquiry, they will already perceive you as a credible resource who can help them.

They will hear from you on a consistent basis. And, the messages you send as well as the scripting you use will clearly communicate the benefits you can provide them. They will, therefore, perceive you as a potentially valuable and worthwhile resource.

I came to realize that there was, in fact, far more sales potential within that group I *couldn't* reach and within the group that I did reach but who said "No" than there was among the group of prospects who immediately agreed to a meeting.

---

8. MORE PROFITS

You get revenues. More accounts. Higher margins.

These rewards are the natural result of a prospecting engine that is running smoothly. You will be meeting with more qualified prospects so you can choose to work with the best and say good-bye to the rest. You can now negotiate from strength on proposals. Why shave the margin to get a piece of business when you know from your full sales pipeline that you are already on target to meet or exceed your sales, revenue and profit goals? You will no longer have to take a lousy account because you are below goal and desperate.

9. YOUR CLOSE RATIO IMPROVES

I once conducted a prospecting intervention for a $100 million company with 27 salespeople. After my coaching intervention, which lasted a few months, the closing ratio of this team increased 25%.

There were two reasons for this increase. Better closing ratios are determined, in part, by the quality of the prospects and the quality of the sales process.

Quality of the prospects: There is a certain pool of prospects that is ideal for your company. You understand their needs, you can service them and keep them happy. The problem is always getting in front of them and being able to tell your story to the right person.

The process introduced to you in this book helped them to infiltrate a much higher percentage of their ideal target group and get in front of the top decision-makers.

Quality of the sales process: Because they were in front of more prospects, this client got more practice and became more proficient at each step of the sales process. They focused on what to do at a first meeting to advance a sale, how to better cross-sell, how to best avoid and respond to resistance and how to improve proposals.

If you get more appointments with widget sellers, you get better at knowing what to do to advance and close a widget deal every step of the way.

10. YOU CAN EASILY FOLLOW-UP

The one thing I hear again and again and again from sales-people is: " *I don't have the time to follow up.*"

No offense. But it is just downright wasteful and insane to spend all that time smiling and dialing... asking questions... and getting tons of information not to follow up.

The biggest investment of time is your initial foray to the prospect. The largest dollar expense that's made is buying the target list, getting it into the database and investing the time to work it.

Easy follow-up is something you plan for before you make your first call.

Follow-up can be simple when you have planned for it and you work with *groups* of prospects.

Many people invest substantial amounts of time and money to start prospecting only to fail to follow up after the initial calls.

That is not going to happen to you. Because at the same time you are calling into companies, you will be coding and segmenting those records. You will be collecting information that enables you to sort and prioritize targets as to potential worth. This is something that takes no additional time and is no expense to you. The result will be that you can launch "touches" (whether they will be letters, emails, postcards, faxes or something else) literally with the touch of a few keystrokes.

3

Success Stories

Who has convinced you that "impossible" to reach decision-makers are impossible to reach and how much is that belief costing you?

Let me give you some examples of results obtained by others using these organization techniques and strategies. Then you decide what they may do for you.

500 MEETINGS FIRST YEAR

This client was a $25 million company in the employee relocation industry. If you had a company with lots of employees and you were transferring executives around the world, you would hire this company to coordinate all aspects of the relocation.

The prospecting target was the VP of personnel or HR at companies having at least 1,000 employees. The client had six outside sales reps. Previously, on 4 different occasions, using 4 different sales consultants, the client had unsuccessfully tried generating qualified meetings for the salesteam by using inside telereps.

The average sale was worth a quarter million dollars a year and the average new account was retained for 3 – 7 years. The client just couldn't seem to get enough qualified meetings no matter what was tried. However, within a year two part-time telemarketers were generating 500 plus meetings annually for the outside reps.

$100 MILLION + CEO'S

Here's one of my favorites. A mid-tier management consulting company with a lot of experience but virtually no name recognition is prospecting for consulting contracts when downsizing was the rage.

Their average consulting contract was worth $500,000.

They knew from experience that when they could initiate the relationship by first meeting with the President or CEO of a company with a minimum of $100,000,000 in sales, they had a conversion rate (of first meetings to a consulting contract) that was at least five times greater than if their initial point of contact was on the Sr. Executive VP level or below.

No mailing was allowed by the consulting firm. The goal was to cold call and penetrate all the "screens" to get the CEO to pick up the phone. Then, in the course of a typical two and a half minute conversation, set up a meeting for one of the outside sales reps.

Using techniques that weren't as advanced as what is described in this book, the result of my work with those consultants was 5+ meetings with CEO's scheduled weekly. I was the one who made those calls and achieved those results working only 12 hours a week.

REVENUE QUADRUPLES IN 18 MONTHS

A home based graphic designer/desktop publishing person who was working way too hard for too little money needed help. She was servicing too many low volume, low margin accounts. But she was soon able to use these techniques to quadruple her business revenues in just 18 months.

How did she do it? By scheduling 65 face-to-face meetings with top decision-makers at companies she had only previously dreamed about having as clients. She converted 8 of those meetings to accounts that generated steady revenue for her. She bought the house she had been renting, and took the family to Disney World. There is now a Lexus parked in the driveway.

$700,000 IN 14 WEEKS

This next project I'm going to tell you about was with a technology company that had 27 people on the sales team. They saw a slump coming and decided to take a proactive approach.

We started with a seminar for the sales team. Then, we produced some custom recorded audiotapes specific to the company needs and distributed the tapes to the sales force. Then, we added personal coaching and company-specific support material into the sales training mix. We started the project right after the first of the year.

By April 16 the VP of Sales told me he had documented $700,000 in closed business (that is: done deals... purchase orders signed... checks received).

These results were directly attributable to sales appointments that would not have been set without the strategies and methods in this book.

Those were just the deals that were closed within the first 14 weeks. There were still a lot more in the pipeline. The company had knowledgeable, talented salespeople who could sell. What they had been lacking were enough effective strategies to get their salespeople in front of more of the right people at those companies they most desired as clients. We solved that problem.

TURNING UP THE GAS ON SALES

This was interesting. Energy deregulation was new a few years back and supplier companies had to learn how to compete. This large electricity and natural gas provider wanted to sell to major companies nationally that spent millions of dollars for energy resources annually.

No lists exist that identify the decision maker for energy purchases in large companies. This is a market that didn't even exist a few years ago. Bottom line – I set up the program and recommended and trained the part-time tele-prospector who set an average of seven qualified meetings a week.

Soon after the program was up and running smoothly and I had moved on, this energy company doubled the compensation of the tele-prospector. They launched with 200 meetings in six months.

THE SYSTEM WAS THE SAME

These examples I've just given represent both large and small companies. They are from diverse industries: consulting, relocation, high tech products and energy. But, the system... the process used to get those results... incorporated the same principles and strategies (with very little variation) that you are learning with this book.

4

Foundation Principles Of Big-Ticket Appointment Setting

Prosper by working within these rules, or waste your time and resources by ignoring them.

Setting sales appointments among top decision makers is challenging work. Virtually no big ticket service or item can be sold without first meeting personally with a top decision maker in the prospect's organization. Those meetings and all the subsequent business that comes from gaining access to top people will flow from your ability to work within, understand and appreciate these foundation principles of appointment-setting success.

Keep something in mind. Most people who attempt to gain access to the very top corporate decision makers are unsuccessful at it. If you follow common wisdom, or if you are inclined to do what everyone else thinks is right, you are doomed to failure. Remember: you want superior — even extraordinary — results. You are never going to get them by laboring under the same misconceptions and doing the same thing as everyone else.

Every action, every script, every call pattern... how you consciously allocate your time... what you will measure... all must

be consistent with certain rules. Know them and thrive. Ignore
them and you will continue to waste your time and miss out on
opportunities that would otherwise be yours.

RULE #1

IN ANY GIVEN POOL OF SUSPECTS, THERE
WILL ONLY BE SO MANY TARGETS THAT ARE
REACHABLE *AND* RECEPTIVE.

That makes sense doesn't it? In any given pool of targets,
there are only going to be so many that would be receptive to
your message if they got a chance to hear it.

Let me give you an example. For any pool of 100 suspects,
you should expect to set meetings with 9% to 13% of the suspect
companies in that pool. So, for purposes of discussion, let's say
the average is 10%. That means in any given pool of 100 targets,
you are going to set about 10 meetings within a few weeks. So
call-call-call... and set meetings 1 through 9.

Now at some point, you have to ask yourself if you are better
off calling a new pool of 100 targets that you know (with a high
degree of probability) contains 10 meetings. Or, do you continue
to call this group of 91 suspects to find the one meeting that is
left?

You always should be aware of and make intelligent decisions as to how you allocate your time. A good part of effective
prospecting and appointment-setting comes down to good time
management. It's about you purposely deciding where to allocate
your time in order to get the greatest leverage for your investment.

If you were to make the conscious decision to call 91 records
in search of one meeting rather than calling 100 records that con-

tain 10 meetings, you'd be misallocating your time. And remember... YOU are in control of your time; not the people you call.

RULE #2

THERE IS A POINT OF DIMINISHING RETURNS FOR ALL OUR ACTIONS

When you are in the sales chase, you must be well aware of your point of diminishing returns. At what point would you be better served by letting go; stopping the chase; and pursuing a new target? If you don't know, you are doomed to failure. Why?

Without that awareness you fall into the trap of spending way too much time on the same group of suspect records... beating your head against the wall and wondering why you get so frustrated. You'll quickly end up convincing yourself that prospecting doesn't seem to work for you. Don't do it.

Start from the beginning with the realization that there are only so many good opportunities to be had in any group. If you accept that (and you should), then logically you should accept two other concepts.

The first: At some point we have to stop beating our heads against the wall and move on.

The second: If there are only so many good opportunities in any given pool of prospects, then you must move through your records at a certain pace in order to consistently achieve good results.

Let me give you an example. I am working a pool of records that statistically gives me one meeting for every 10 targets with whom I initiate my process. That process starts when I make an initial call into a company and identify the decision maker. That is the beginning of a pre-determined call process.

By definition then, if I need 5 meetings a week to meet my sales objectives, then I must initiate my process with 50 new targets a week. (Remember? I set one meeting for every 10 suspect companies with whom I identify the top decision maker and complete my predetermined successful prospecting process. 10 x 5 = 50) Less than 50 and I have <u>no chance</u> of setting an average of 5 sales appointments weekly.

This also means that, on average, I have to identify decision makers at 10 new target companies every day. If I do not do that, then it means that I will soon be making calls to the same people over and over again. That is a certain recipe for disaster. Why?

There are only so many suspects in any given pool of targets who are reachable and would be receptive to our request if we reach them. Once they are reached, if we continue to call what remains of that pool, we are beating a dead horse. Once most of those who would be receptive to our message have been reached and agreed to a meeting, we are choosing to work with records with which there is a very low probability of success, if at all.

It doesn't matter whether you're calling company CEO's, top VP's, mega companies... or middle sized companies... doesn't matter... one appointment set for every 10 suspect companies called seems to be pretty much the result obtained consistently.

Well, if you are an appointment setter who doesn't want to keep banging his/her head against the wall, you have to know where your point of diminishing returns is. If your calling program gets one appointment set for every 10 records, you have some choices to make that will determine your productivity. If you have 100 targeted suspect companies and can expect 10 appointments... that means that as you call this pool and schedule 4, 5 or 6 appointments, you can expect less from your efforts as you continue working that pool. When you schedule appointment number 8, you have to be thinking to yourself... where am I better off? I have scheduled 8 appointments in this pool of 100. I can keep calling the remaining 92 records looking for probably 2 appointments.... or I can drop these turkeys and call a fresh group of 100. At least I'd know with probability there would be 10 new appointments. What would you rather do... call 92 records to find 2 appointments or call 100 records to find 10 appointments? Remember, you are in charge and you get to choose.

So just to summarize: there are only so many meetings in any group; you must let go at some time; you must always be aware of your point of diminishing returns; and your system must have flow (this means you are always initiating your process with a pre-determined number of new records, while at the same time you make a conscious decision to stop calling those that have reached the point of diminishing returns). If you don't stop at the point of diminishing returns, you won't have the time to start calling the new pool of records that contain many more new appointments.

RULE #3

THE REASON MOST PEOPLE DON'T AGREE TO MEET WITH US IS THAT WE DON'T GIVE THEM *ENOUGH* REASON TO MEET WITH US.

If you are connecting with people on the phone and they are not receptive to your message, this is happening for the simple reason that you have not given them enough reason to agree. You haven't provided enough reason for them to invest 30, 45 or 60 minutes of their time with you.

Every single word you say counts. Every-single-word. And, you have a very limited time on the phone to state your case. It has been proven that people think 10 times faster than they listen. So don't go babbling on with unnecessary words in the very limited time you have to get a suspect's attention. Your target is thinking while you blabber... probably thinking: "this person is

just like all the rest... a waste of time I'm going to get rid of."
Once a target comes to that conclusion, nothing you say will dislodge them from the belief that you have nothing worth their time.

So what do you do? First, write down what you plan to say so that you can make every word you use as powerful as possible. Eliminate everything that is unrelated to communicating a benefit and a reason to meet. And understand this: the benefit they get from meeting you has to be delivered at the initial meeting.

The biggest reason suspects don't meet with you is because you don't give them <u>enough</u> reason to meet with you. But... they are much more likely to meet with you if they know that <u>at the first meeting,</u> they are going to get something they consider to be worthwhile regardless of whether or not they do business with you in the future.

Are you structuring your pitch to tell suspects (essentially) that you are great, do great stuff, and want to meet so you can find out more about them to determine how you can assist them so you can come back to them at a later date with something specific? That is just not as powerful as telling them that you have information and strategies about how similar companies have solved the same kind of problems and achieved similar goals that the suspect's firm would like to achieve. And, the best part is that you are going to provide this information and those strategies at the time of the first meeting.

Strip out every unnecessary word. Tell them clearly and concisely how they will benefit when they meet you the first time. Chapter 15 provides you specific examples of how this is done.

RULE #4

YOUR SYSTEM MUST BE
SUSTAINABLE AND DUPLICABLE

In reality, most people who start to prospect (even if they get off to a good start) stop somewhere along the way. They get busy... or bored and frustrated with a lack of results. So they stop.

Not a good thing if you want more good-quality profitable accounts. Many times I believe that people stop prospecting because they just don't get the results they think they need to justify their time. Or, they spend too much money relative to the results they do get. Sometimes they just can't see the big picture of how their current activity will impact their paycheck, career or company in the future.

If you use strategies that get you short term results but cost too much on a per inquiry or per meeting basis, you won't want to continue and the system isn't sustainable. If you have to spend too much time to get a meeting scheduled, the system isn't sustainable.

Your system must be sustainable in the sense that you know that if you invest a certain amount of time and money that you will cost-effectively get a result you seek. When your system is sustainable, you will know that as you progress, the system enables you to segment and code your targets and utilize the information you pick up during your calls so that you will be motivated to continue its use.

In addition to being sustainable, it must be duplicable. It must be duplicable in the sense that you could train a co-worker to use the system. Such a person might take over where you left off... or work the process on a whole new group of targets thereby giving your business even more opportunities.

Your system must be duplicable because it is very likely that there will come a time when you are spending so much time attending the meetings that you schedule and following up on those opportunities, that you now find it difficult to make time to prospect. And, human nature being what it is, let's face the fact that if you have other things to do, it is usually prospecting that will be neglected. You can't let that happen if you want to ensure a continuous flow of solid, worthwhile new business opportunities coming to you.

If your system is duplicable, you can pass the calling duties on to someone else. You can duplicate the system and delegate to a lower level of competence.

I have seen many companies start a campaign by having some of the salespeople implement the prospecting system with success. But once results came in, they quickly realized that they needed to have the higher paid salespeople on the road selling all the time while others (paid at a lower rate) could handle the prospecting and appointment setting function more than adequately.

RULE #5

WHEN APPOINTMENT SETTING, YOU MUST THINK IN TERMS OF GROUPS, NOT INDIVIDUALS

Always think of success in terms of groups rather than individual records. If you think in terms of individual records you are doomed to failure. The vast majority of people you try to communicate with will be unreachable, have no need or say "no." So, it will be rejection rejection rejection.

The big picture must be based not how you do with any specific target, but how well you do with any particular **group** of targets.

Are you going to choose to invest 10 hours of time working a group of records that you know usually contains two meetings? Or, are you going to invest 10 hours of time to work a group of records that you know statistically contains 8 meetings?

Let's put it another way. Are you going to invest 10 hours of your time working a group of records that results in an average sale of $50,000 or a group of records that results in an average sale of $250,000? Are you going to invest time with a group of records with a typical 3 month sales cycle or a group of records with a typical 9 month sales cycle?

You must also be aware of groups that are just not responsive by nature or within which you are likely to have a lower probability of success. You must be able to identify these groups so that you can avoid them.

A very dangerous group of suspects is that group that requests information or asks that you call them back. Many neophyte prospectors believe that these are positive signs. In reality, this just lets the targets control their time and then they call call call and wonder why they are not getting anywhere close to a real appointment.

If you are working with any group of records and discovering that you are not getting results with that group, change your strategy with that group to be more effective.

The *"send me some info"* request is almost always a blow off and a time waster. If ten people wish to end a call with a "send me some info" request, maybe one or two at most, is a legitimate prospect worth your follow-up time. So, being well aware of the big picture and knowing that most follow-up time on a general request for more info is going to be a complete waste of time, you can include strategies in your call process to separate that group of targets who would request information just to get rid of you and have no legitimate need or intention of buying, from that group of targets that request information because they do have a legitimate need and may buy. Therefore, they are worth an additional time investment.

Remember – Rule #5 says that you should think about success in terms of groups rather than individuals. Here's an example of how that would work.

You might decide that for best results you will invest 50% of your calling time on that class of targets that makes a buying decision within 90 days so that you can guarantee a reasonably steady cash flow. And then you might use the other 50% of your time for that class of prospects that offers a much larger, more profitable sale but typically takes 9 months to complete a sales cycle.

When you think in terms of groups and make conscious decisions as to where you will invest your very limited prospecting time, you have greater control over your own business destiny.

RULE #6
YOU MUST OVERCOME GRAVITY

The most common, natural knee jerk reaction that a decision maker usually has to a teleprospector's request to schedule a meeting is "forgetaboutit."

For you to achieve the purpose of your call, you have to "reverse gravity." In order to break free from the gravity that holds prospects down, you must project a more powerful force.

What you say and how you say it must contain enough positive energy to overcome a decision maker's normal, natural reaction to not schedule a meeting with you. You will only overcome that if you take calculated actions, are prepared and **practice**.

RULE #7
YOU MUST ALWAYS RETAIN CONTROL

Your targets should not control what you do. You control what you do. Always be in control of the conversation. Always steer a conversation that wanders off-course back to your purpose. Always be in control of where you invest your time and your resources

If your targets are in control, you are doomed to failure. Example: We made reference to the typical "*send me some info*" or "*call me back*" blow off. Well, if you put a smile on your face and readily agree to such requests you will have lost control. Your targets will now be in control of your time and you will most certainly lose.

When we get into scripting and responses to resistance, you will learn strategies to maintain control in such instances. Always be in control of the conversation and how you invest your time.

RULE #8
FOCUS ONLY ON THOSE
WHO WOULD BE RECEPTIVE TO YOUR MESSAGE.
IGNORE EVERYONE ELSE

People who have no needs, no money or no time will be annoyed and bothered regardless of what you do. Their feelings are totally irrelevant. Your objective - your *sole* objective - is to get the most out of the time/money that you invest in prospecting (to schedule the most appointments with qualified prospects as you can).

For your company and yourself, you cannot let those who have no needs that you can satisfy dictate your actions. Focus only on how to deliver your message effectively to those who *do* have a need. So, at the moment of truth when you only have a couple of seconds to deliver your carefully calculated, benefit-rich message, these prospects will absorb it and be receptive to it.

Always speak and act as if you were speaking to someone who would be receptive to your message.

What do I mean by this?

What is one of the biggest forms of resistance that I hear from new trainees? "Well I don't want to leave another message so soon. I don't want to be a pest. I don't want to turn them off." Surer words that predict prospecting failure I have never heard.

You have to think only of those who you can reach; who have a need; and who, if they can clearly comprehend and absorb the major benefits you can deliver to them, would agree to meet with you. Ignore everyone else.

Focus only on actions that would be welcomed by those who are reachable, have a need and would be receptive to meeting with you.

True story. A friend of mine was sitting in his living room enjoying and relaxing the day by watching a ball game. The door bell rings... he thinks: oh no... a solicitor... somebody trying to

---

Well, the great majority of people we speak to have no need or desire to buy what we are selling. That being the case, many salespeople water down what they have to say in order to be comfortable with this class of prospects that they anticipate will say no.

They don't want to bother or interrupt people. They don't want to annoy them (whatever that means). This is a ridiculous thought. Of course you want to interrupt people. You want to interrupt them and get them to focus on you.

sell me something... a neighbor wants me to sign a petition... I'll ignore them and they will go away... ring ring ring... bang bang bang. My buddy is thinking: what a nerve they have bothering me like this... I'll just ignore them and they will go away. The person at the front door now moves over to the side door... ring ring ring... bang bang bang. My buddy is now annoyed, aggravated, bothered, and *determined* to ignore them because he assumes they have nothing that interests him and he is not going to waste his time.

Ring ring ring; bang bang bang... next my buddy hears banging on the slider window in his living room. Now he is infuriated by the nerve of this person who just doesn't get the message. So, he gets up and walks over to the slider window to see a person frantically waving his arms yelling, "Mr. Mr. - your roof is on fire!"

Did my buddy have a need? Was that message welcomed?

Everything you say and how you say it must assume that you are speaking to someone who has a need and will be willing (as well as able) to buy from you as soon as you've educated them a little.

You have a very limited time to make your case before the minds of suspects' and prospects' shut off and they conclude that you are wasting their time.

Don't waste precious time probing to see if they have a need or interest before you unload the heavy guns and deliver your powerful benefit-laden message. Don't ask decision makers who don't know you "if they have a few minutes"? Waste no words that don't communicate benefits to those who need what you offer. Deliver only words that communicate benefits to them. Deliver only the words that would get someone who has a need you can fill to sit up and pay attention to you.

RULE #9

"YOU CAN'T MAKE A SILK PURSE OUT OF A SOW'S EAR." (LOOK ONLY FOR YOUR NEW CLIENTS.)

Look for your new clients only. Discard everybody else. Have you ever heard of the phrase: "you can't make a silk purse out of a sow's ear?" Well, you have to have the confidence to know that there are plenty of great new clients are out there for you

If they don't recognize a need, don't have the money, don't have the time to focus… they are not your client, and no amount of wishful thinking will change that.

Most of your best clients fit a certain profile. They respond a certain way to your calls and move through your sales pipeline pretty much like all your other good clients did. The more you vary from your desirable new account profile or an appointment setting or sales process that works, the less results you will obtain.

Assuming you have picked the right pool of targets, all you have to do is move methodically through that pool and deliver a very clear precise benefit-laden message. When you do, the ears of your future new clients will pick up and they will identify themselves to you. If you are clearly and concisely delivering a benefit-laden message to the right audience, they will respond.

If they do not, maybe you are not being clear and concise. Maybe you are not communicating enough benefits that they are interested in. Or, maybe you have poorly defined the pool of targets that you have chosen to work with.

RULE #10

THE "RULE OF 7"

The rule of 7 states that people have to be touched by us 7 times before we can reasonably expect them to appreciate, understand and respond to our communications.

Now, the rule of 7 is not literal. Some people, when they are first exposed to our message, will respond favorably... as if they had found the holy grail. Others may have to be "touched" dozens of times before they finally respond at all.

The significance of the rule of 7 is twofold. First, if you are not touching your contacts multiple times within a call cycle, you are not touching them at all. If you think you are accomplishing something by calling them and leaving a voicemail message or talking to them once, you are fooling yourself.

Built into your prospecting system must be the core concept that you have to touch people multiple times within a very short period of time to have any chance of getting their attention and an appointment. If your call process doesn't plan on touching your prospects about 7 times, you have no right to expect to get their attention and get an appointment.

How do we touch them? Well, we really only have a few tools at our disposal. Phone. Voicemail. Fax.

Mail is not a viable touch mechanism. It's too expensive and it's too time consuming. In every single instance in which I have seen an individual or company use the mail as part of their prospecting program, they have lost their shirt.

If the rule of 7 says that you have to touch people 7 times before they really start to get it, how long should it take you to deliver those touches?

> **Most business executives get stacks and stacks of mail…
> and they throw most of it away with hardly a glance. Yet
> somehow, these same executives are convinced that the
> mail they send out will get noticed… studied… and some-
> how have people anticipating their phone call. Absolute
> foolishness!**

Let's think about this. If it takes 7 touches for your target to
be impacted and you called and left a message every couple of
weeks it would take 14 weeks to deliver 7 touches. Do you really
want to wait 14 weeks to have impact and know whether your
target is a viable prospect? I don't think so.

So, what if you were to deliver another touch? Send a fax
whenever you leave a voicemail message. That's another touch.
Two touches at once every couple of weeks. That's better. Now it
would only take 3 weeks to complete your cycle.

But I have a call sequence that's even better for you. From
experience, I can tell you that if you space out your touches over
too long a period of time, it is kind of like starting over again
every time.

Anything done once is the equivalent of doing nothing at all.
Setting appointments is an assault. It takes constant, consistent
and calculated action to have a chance of getting someone's attention… never mind their agreement to meet with you. If you do
something once.. one call.. one fax… and think you have done
something to further your business objective you are deluding
yourself.

People don't remember. You need cumulative impact. You
need people to be touched numerous times within a short enough
period of time so that they recognize you are trying to communicate with them. If they recognize that… you have a chance… a
chance… that they may absorb your message and be more predis-
posed to receiving your call.

You need the impact of cumulative touches and spaced repetition to penetrate into the minds of your targets.

What works best? Deliver your touches over roughly a two week period. Send your targets a series of faxes and voicemails. Do this and you increase the impact of your actions. You are consistently sending a benefit rich message to your carefully-chosen targets.

If they have a need for your product or service, you have greatly increased the odds that they will respond or be more receptive to your message.

You are going to make a lot of phone calls, leave a lot of voicemails, and send a lot of faxes. You want maximum impact for your actions. Live by the rule of 7 and deliver those touches within a two week window.

Not only must we touch people multiple times before we have a right to expect them to respond, but we must remember that the flip side of that activity is closely related to the law of diminishing returns.

If we are sending our clear concise benefit-rich communications to the right audience, and if they have been touched by us multiple times within a short period of time but have not responded, then we can safely conclude that they are not our next clients. They have no needs we can fulfill. We should move on.

So, with the rule of 7, we build into our system multiple touches so that we can realistically expect a response from those who recognize a need we might meet. With those multiple touches we can have the confidence to let go when there is no response. If these suspects had a need, our system of multiple voicemail and faxes that have been delivered within a short period of time would have maximized the chance that they will become aware of our core benefits and "raise their hand" from the crowd. When they don't, we can move on with confidence.

RULE #11

THE *"RULE OF 60/30/10"*

This is also a great rule to keep yourself on track. The rule states that 60% of your prospecting success will come simply by hitting the right targets, 30% will come because you have the right message and 10% will come from all other reasons combined.

This is a critical rule. I can guarantee you that if you have an ineffective prospecting program, you are not hitting the right targets. And, you probably don't deliver a message that has impact on your targets.

60% of your results come from just hitting the right targets. Here's a big mistake I see over and over again. You have the urge to "do something." Rather than carefully profile the best targets for you to call, you grab some local list that is free or easy (or, you rent something quickly) and start calling. Then you wonder why you get no results.

Even if you have an average message and screw everything else up totally, if you select the right targets, you can have a successful prospecting program. If you select the wrong targets... no matter what you do, no matter how good your message is, no matter how efficiently you work, no matter how good your materials are, you are absolutely guaranteed to fail.

How do you pick the right targets? Very simple. Make a list of your best clients. Make a list of your competition's best clients. Make a list of the specific accounts that you know would be great, profitable accounts for you to have. Then go to a database and look up those specific companies. Create a chart that notes their SIC number (standard industry code).

Every industry has a code. Do you sell to consultants, restaurants or retail? They each have a code. Find out what the SIC codes are of the companies you are profiling. Make note of their size. (Usually you will make this judgment by revenue range or employee size.) This information is also found in publicly available databases. Note their zip code to determine where they are geographically.

Apart from information you find in public databases, make note of how your best clients/customers/accounts first found you. What needs did they have when they first became your clients? Write it down. What did they tell you their problems were when they first came to you? Write them down.

Do this enough times, and you will have an accurate profile of the people whom you should be calling. That is to say you will clearly know the exact industry codes and the size of the businesses you should be calling. You will also know precisely where they are located geographically. These are the **only** people you should be calling.

DO NOT FOCUS ON "NOT MISSING ANYONE."

The point of prospecting isn't to "not miss anyone." The point of prospecting and appointment setting is to generate the most results for your limited time and resources.

When you start, you should call only those that fit the profile of your best potential clients. Usually, there are more of those targets than you could reasonably call in six months or more. So, you are not limiting yourself in any way. After you contact all your targets that fit your "best suspect" profile, and do it very well, then you can start thinking about contacting others.

Let me tell you where the self-destructive thinking usually comes from. We all have clients whom are great clients who we love but who don't fit the profile of our very best clients. For example: if most of our best clients are businesses that have at least $2.5 million in revenue, we probably have some great clients that are much smaller only doing say half of a million or a million a year in business. Fight the urge to mix the smaller companies into your target pool initially. It will doom you to failure. Focus only on those who fit within your "best target" profile. After you finish working your best target pool, you can test and determine if another target pool outside of those parameters can be prospected cost-effectively.

> **Let me tell you one of the biggest mistakes you can make. The phrase that I hear that tells me I am talking to someone doomed to prospecting failure...** *"I don't want to miss anyone."* **Surer words predicting failure will never be uttered!**

It may be true that there are some businesses out there that only do half a million dollars in revenue who could be *"great"* clients. But, if you tried to prospect companies in that revenue range, you would lose your shirt trying to find the "great" clients.

You are not "giving up" on anyone when you resist the temptation to dilute the quality of the suspect pool you call.

It is financial suicide and sheer madness to invest limited prospecting time sifting through sludge panning for a few small nuggets of gold, when you could spend the same amount of time jack hammering through a vein of gold containing many more larger nuggets.

Only an idiot would say "I don't want to miss any small nuggets" to justify ignoring a spot where much more could be found.

The more you vary from a suspect pool that most resembles your typical "great" client, the more you can expect that your success rate in scheduling appointments will be lower. Your conversion rate from appointment to sale will be lower, and your average order size of the sales you do make will be lower. Do not make this mistake. Initially focus and prospect only those companies who fit the profile of your very best clients.

Once you finish prospecting that pool and have a baseline of results, you can then selectively start prospecting other pools of suspects.

60% of your results will come just from communicating with the right targets. 30% of your prospecting results come from communicating the right message. 10% comes from everything else.

RULE #12

MAKE EVERY WORD COUNT. RUTHLESSLY ELIMINATE EVERY UNNECESSARY WORD.

When you are trying to set a sales appointment, you have very limited time to get someone's attention and relay benefits in such a way that they will agree to spend an hour or so with you. You have to know specifically what words are most likely to get you the result you seek.

You have to think about it and you have to write those words down. Every word counts. If you take 50 seconds to say something that could have been said in 30 seconds, you will lose a lot of appointments. If you don't clearly communicate the most powerful benefits that you offer before someone says "no," you will lose a lot of appointments.

Most people will agree with me up to this point. The next point is where people start to get fuzzy and resistant. My advice is to write down those words and master how you deliver them. That means you are initially going to work from scripts. You have to write down the sequence of words most calculated to get you the result you seek and learn to deliver them effectively.

Remember: 60% of your results come from picking the right targets and 30 % of your results come from delivering the right message. 10% comes from everything else.

Don't get side tracked. I find that people spend very little, if any, time on selecting the right targets. Most won't spend the time to write down the best words to use to set an appointment. Yet, they will spend oodles of time doing things that have very little relationship to results. They will ponder what font to use, or endlessly research all sorts of crazy stuff on companies they haven't even talked to and endlessly search the internet for information that might help them.

Sound familiar? Stop it. Call the right companies. Use the best words.

RULE #13

THE *"80/20 RULE"* – WITH A TWIST.

Everybody has heard of the Pareto principle which states that 80% of our results come from 20% of our efforts. That seems to be true in life and it is certainly true when you set sales appointments.

You can choose to spend substantial amounts of time engaging in activities like calling, voice mailing, and faxing that you know with certainty has a much lower chance of success when compared to other activities.

You can choose to spend substantial amounts of time engaging in activities like calling, voice mailing and faxing that you know with certainty has a much higher chance of success when compared to other activities.

The key phrase here is "you can choose" to engage in those activities ... or not. In order to set appointments effectively, you must know with a relative degree of certainty what to expect from calls and contacts made to segments of your list.

You must come to know how many appointments are set per record called... what the conversion rate to sales will be...and what the average sale size is.

You can choose to work only in the zone in which you get 80% of your results from only 20% of your time or ..... you can choose to work in the zone where you get 20% of your results with 80% of your effort. It's your choice.

The reason why I think so many people get frustrated by prospecting and appointment setting is that they spend way too much time in that lower probability of results zone and too little of their time in that higher probability of results zone. You can decide where to spend your time.

RULE #14

BE DIFFERENT

Why? Most sales appointment setting programs fail.

That is to say: most people who try to set sales appointments consistently, get bored, get frustrated or just plain give up on prospecting..

If you do what most people do… if you succumb to common thoughts about what is the "right thing" to do…. you will fail.

Why would you expect to do what everyone else does… and get drastically different results?

Implement a program that works and see your business grow. Don't pay attention to what others say.

RULE #15

REMOVE THE DRUDGERY

This system is set up so that you can move quickly through a prospect pool delivering a carefully calculated message with impact and get a yes or no with certainty. This removes the drudgery.

Drudgery occurs when you make wasted calls... when you enter needless notes into your system... when you are not delivering your touches... and when you purposely engage in double-shoveling (doing things twice when you only have to do them once). It is all drudgery and you are the one creating it. Stop it.

RULE #16

"NO" IS A PERFECTLY ACCEPTABLE RESULT. (THE "MAYBE'S" WILL KILL YOU).

"NO" is a perfectly acceptable result.

In fact, getting to a "NO" as quickly as possible is one of the things you **have** to do in order to excel at appointment setting. Many people will do anything to avoid getting a "no". But, that also means that you are not direct and getting enough "yes" answers.

Success in the appointment setting game has an awful lot to do with how quickly you can move through a pool of records effectively. When you move through those records, you need to know things with certainty. This is a "yes." This is a "no." Or, if you couldn't reach targets, your process of multiple and consistently focused touches delivered within a short period of time should give you the confidence to conclude that if they had a need there was plenty of opportunity for them to "raise their hand" out of the crowd. Once you reach that conclusion, move on.

Those who are best at prospecting for gold are best at identifying that which is *not* gold. The faster you can get a clear and concise "No," the sooner you'll recognize what's "not gold." And that means you will spend less time with people who are unlikely to meet with you, and more time with those more likely to meet with you.

It is not the "no's" you should be afraid of. It is the "maybe's" that will keep you from prospecting success. "Maybe's" are multiple conversations with someone who conveys warm fuzzies yet never agrees to meet. You **must** avoid the "maybe's." Be direct. Be professional. Get a clear yes or no.

5

What To Say

Preparation, practice, written scripts and <u>benefits </u>are the keys to delivering the most powerful words

Now the time has arrived to figure out exactly what you are going to say.

You have to sit down and write out some scripts. Why is it necessary for you to work from a script? Because you have very little time on the phone and every second counts.

If it takes you 40 seconds to say things you could say in 30 seconds you will lose opportunities. If your decision-maker tunes you out because your opening is not good or you haven't given a good enough reason to listen in the first 3 seconds, you will lose those opportunities. If you don't convey all the things that are necessary so that your target will agree to talk to you a bit more or decide to go to the next step with you, you will lose opportunities.

On the phone everything is compressed by a factor of about 10. When you are face to face with people, they might indulge you a few minutes of small talk before they expect you to get to the point. Or, they conclude that you are wasting their time and discount you totally. But on the phone, that takes only seconds.

In a face to face meeting, prospects might give you 30 or 40 minutes of attention to state your case. On the phone, however, you only get a few moments to state your case and reach your objective. So if you are not prepared (meaning that you have planned in advance how to make maximum use of every precious second to state your case and get where you need to go), you will lose opportunities.

Now, let me also say something else very bluntly. When planning out what you have to say to reach your objectives, you have to assume that every person you will speak to has a need that you can fill. The words you use must be structured to reach your business objective with those who have a need you can fill (even though most of them, in fact, will not have a need you can fill). Totally disregard everyone else. Let me say that again. Focus only on those who have a need you can fill. **Totally** disregard everyone else.

The reality is that most of the people we choose as suspects and most of the people we will have conversations with do not have a need we can fill. They are going to say "no"; "not at this time"; or "take me off your list."

If we water down the words we use to have more comfortable conversation with those who do not have needs we can fill, we will be less effective when we say "Hello" to a top quality prospect who has a need we can fill.

When a top quality prospect who has a need we can fill picks up the phone and says "Hello," at that moment we don't know they have a need we can fill and they don't know what we can provide them or just how capable and credible we are.

Within 3 seconds, that top decision maker will determine whether you are worth listening to for a few more moments. What are you going to say? "Hi. This is Pauline Prospector from Mega Corporation. Did I catch you at a bad time? Do you have a few moments"? Do those words give someone who has a need that you can fill… cause for pause? What have you done to cause a great future account to focus on you just a little bit longer, rather than cut you short?

Most calls from prospective vendors waste our time. We know that and immediately treat them accordingly. What are you going to do to avoid the possibility that a great future account for you, someone who wants and needs what you can provide, snarls at you or voices displeasure at the interruption before they cut you short and hang up?

I once had the opportunity to work with a new trainee who was working very hard but just couldn't seem to put it together and get some consistent traction in sales. He resisted the idea of being direct and calling people in sequence to "touch" them 7 times within a short period of time so he'd be sure to get their attention. He would say to me (as do many young starving trainees)… *"but I am afraid I am going to annoy them."* Annoy them?

You must do what you have to in order to get the attention of those who have a need you can fill. These are the people who, if they received the right information about all the benefits you could provide, would trade you 30-60 minutes of their time to hear about them. That is what you must do. **Focus only** on that.

Stop worrying about the vast majority of people you will contact who don't have a need. Worry only about communicating effectively with those prospects who **do** have a need. By the

---

Those who have no need or are displeased by the interruption will still have no need and be displeased after they know what you might do for them. They are no worse off. However, if you structure your script so that within the first few seconds you give them …. cause for pause, 100% of those who could be great future accounts of yours, will continue to listen to what you have planned to say.

way… that trainee whom I mentioned above washed out… just like everyone else I have worked with who has voiced the same thoughts.

You will need three basic scripts.

• Your Identify The Decision Maker Script

• Your Set The Meeting Script

• Your Voicemail Script.

In order to achieve the purpose intended, those scripts have to be structured in a certain way.

YOUR IDENTIFY THE DECISION MAKER SCRIPT

Let's consider the first script I call the "Identify The Decision Maker" script. Let's assume you have a list of companies that you have decided to prospect and you don't know who the decision-maker is or you have a name you think is the decision-maker but you have to confirm it.

Now let's set the scene up. You are calling into Mega Corporation and you are probably going to get the main receptionist who is handling too many incoming calls and some administrative chores as well. Your objective on this first call is to identify the decision-maker, obtain his/her fax number and permission to fax, and hopefully some sorting information. That is it.

Your objective is not to talk to them. Your objective is only to get the information you need so you can move to the next step in the appointment setting process. Let's assume that you don't have a name and you are gunning for the person who makes marketing and advertising decisions.

Step 1: Get the name.

You call and the overwhelmed receptionist picks up the phone:

Receptionist: "Thank you for calling Mega Corp how can I help you?"

Prospector: "I'd like to send some information to whomever handles your marketing and advertising. Can you tell me who to direct it to?"

Or

" I was looking to send some information to whomever handles the purchase of your computers or technology equipment. Can you tell me who to direct it to?"

Or

" Hi I was looking to send some information to your Vice President of Sales. Could you tell me who to direct it to?"

Or

"Hi, I was looking to send some information to whomever handles employee relocations. Can you tell me who to direct that to?"

Now, let's think about this for a moment. Most salespeople call companies to speak to decision makers. It is the receptionists' job to protect these decision makers from harassment. But, you are indicating that all you want to do is send them some information.

Now, what do you think the overwhelmed receptionist is thinking? All this person wants to do is send some information that is going to be thrown away anyway… so the receptionist figures: "*sure no problem.*"

Because you are not acting very much like a typical aggressive salesperson, but are acting very nonchalant (almost uncaring about the answer). You will get the name you want with the first call 19 out of 20 times.

So, if you don't have a name, the sequences is like this:

Receptionist: "Hello. Mega Corporation. How may I help you"?

Teleprospector: "*Hi. I was looking to send some information to your MIS director. Could you tell me who to send it to?*"

That script is very direct and <u>tells receptionists exactly what it is that you want</u>. There is no doubt whatsoever as to what you want so they can give you the answer you want. Do not add words. Don't ask how they are. Don't make comments about the weather or other irrelevancies.

Usually they will say… "*Send it to Cindy Server*" You immediately act to obtain the next bit of information you need without wasting a syllable.

Step 2: Get the fax number.

You immediately say "<u>Thanks would you mind if I faxed that</u>?

They always say "*Sure that's OK*" and then you say "*what is that fax number?*" They give it to you and you follow up with still one more question if you can.

Step 3: The "potential worth" question.

Now, you say: "Great! Hey, just so I know what to send... about how many employees are there with the company now?" More times than not they will tell you 50, 100, 500 whatever.

Or, another option is: "Great. Just so I know what to send, do you have any idea how many salespeople there are with the company?"

The idea is to ask a question which enables you to start the sorting process. In addition to setting sales appointments *now*, you want to obtain the information necessary to obtain more sales appointments *later*, and implement even more effective marketing and sales strategies.

With every call you should be thinking what bit of information you can extract that will help you separate the high-potential opportunities from the average opportunities from the low priority or total waste of time opportunities.

As you call and your pool of identified high-potential opportunities grows, you will be able to allocate more time and more resources toward them and implement strategies more appropriate for that group.

As you make more and more of these first calls, your pool of low priority and no opportunity companies will grow. You can be sure not to waste any additional time or money on this group.

What's missing?

Notice anything interesting about this "Identify The Decision Maker" script? Did I identify myself or the company I am calling from? No! Why?

There are really three reasons I don't identify myself on an Identify The Decision Maker call. First, I have found that I can get the same result without identifying myself as when I do identify myself. Frankly, making these calls is not the most favorite thing I have to do in this world. So, every word I can cut out and every second of boredom or tedium I can eliminate from my life, the better.

Second, receptionists and "gatekeepers" have their antennae up for anyone who is going to make them look bad or harass their superiors. The more information you give them, the more information they possess to conclude that they should screen you out.

In fact, you should make this call with the most bored, nonchalant, and non-caring attitude that you can muster. The bored part should be no problem.

Third, most salespeople (particularly those new to sales) who identify themselves and/or their company to a receptionist immediately raise a red flag that identifies them as exactly the type of person receptionists don't want to cooperate with.

"Hi this is Scott Channell from Breakaway Growth Strategies how are you today? That's great! Weather treating you right down there is it? That's great! Say, I was looking to speak to your vice president of sales. Could you tell me who that is?" Pleasssseeeee. Can't you just hear the click now?

Don't red flag yourself. Be simple. Be direct. Be nonchalant. Get your info. Hang up. Click.

DEFINING FIRST CALL SUCCESS

So let's look at what we accomplished with that initial call. We identified the name of our target; we obtained the fax number; and we got permission to fax the target. Most of the time, we were able to obtain some type of qualifying information as well. We did all that with one call and 19 times out of 20 we will be similarly successful.

Why are those things important to get at this stage? Well as to the fax, go back to the Rule of 7. People don't understand that we are trying to communicate with them nor do they begin to absorb our message until they have been touched by us numerous times. The reality is that most people we plan to dial will not pick up the phone when we try to get through to them. But, if we send a fax in addition to leaving a voicemail message, we can (with minimal additional effort and virtually the same investment of time) deliver two touches rather than one. The more touches, the greater our chance of success.

Because your fax will be structured in such a way that prospects can flag their interest to you without having to pick up the phone, you will get people who will fax back to you. They might fax back an information or meeting request. The fax may lead them to your website page where they can request information or a meeting. They may fax back to opt-in to your E-mail or snail mail list.

On the other hand, they may fax back to tell you to get lost and not contact them again, which is also a desired result (no kidding).

The point is that people can enter your sales pipeline in other ways than agreeing to a meeting on the phone. Fax can make it happen.

I will, in fact, predict that about 20% of your meetings or quote opportunities will come as a direct result of your faxing.

Why wouldn't they? If you hit the right targets with a very clear, benefit-rich message and make it very easy for them to respond, they will do so. I also suggest that you think of it like this… by using the fax you are getting a 20% boost in results with virtually no additional effort.

Remember, it's also important to attempt to get some type of qualifying information on every call. The reality is that with most dials you make you are not going to connect with your target. That doesn't mean it is a wasted call. You can still improve the quality of your calls and direct more of your time toward higher return prospects if you can improve the quality of the information you are working with.

In the previous example the qualifying question might be, *"Oh, just so I know what to send, about how many employees are there in your company?"*

If a company with a thousand or more employees is a much better prospect than a company with 100 employees, you can get that information and allocate your time accordingly. As you identify more and more companies that fit your high priority target profile, you can allocate more calling time to them.

At one time, I used to do a lot of work in the relocation industry for companies that moved top corporate executives all over the world. Obviously, a company doing 250 moves or more a year was a much better potential target than a company doing 25 moves a year. In the sales training business the potential worth question is, *"Just so I know what to send approximately how many salespeople are there in the company?"* You get the answer and invest your time accordingly.

What is your potential worth question?

THE "SET THE MEETING" SCRIPT

Consider this situation. After making a lot of initial calls to identify decision makers and then a lot of follow up calls to get them to pick up the phone, a decision maker whom you are targeting actually picks up the phone. Your objective is to obtain an agreement for that person to meet with you. Let me give you two variations of a "Set The Meeting" script.

Script number one:

Target: "Hello"

Prospector: "This is Pauline Prospector from Super Service Group. We specialize in providing widgets, wadgets, hardware design and implementation services. Companies like Mega Corp, Brito Corporation, and International Amalgamated work with us due to our expertise, quick response and competitive pricing. If you are looking for information or options regarding your widgets, wadgets or equipment supplier, we would like to introduce ourselves and provide information on a few things we do different that have proven valuable. Would you have any time in the next week or two?"

Now, it is typical that you will have to work through a number of scripts before you settle upon the one that gets the results you want. Your "comfort" with the script has nothing to do with whether you will use it or not.

Script number two:

Target: "Hello"

Prospector: "This is Paul Prospector from Super Service Group. We specialize in helping companies select widgets, wadgets and gizmos which best meet their needs. Companies like L. L. Beanstock, Enginola and I. B. Sorry, use us because we are experts and our prices are very competitive. I have no idea if you might be looking for information or options regarding technology equipment. If you are, we would like the opportunity to introduce ourselves, give you some information and strategies to improve delivery time and reduce costs. If you hear something you like and think of us in the future, that would be great. Would you have any time in the next week or two?"

Understand that in order to set an appointment, there is an impression you have to convey that you realistically think your target is going to agree to a meeting. The less you convey this impression, the less successful you will be.

2 Rules For Successful First Conversations

Not only do you have to convey certain impressions but you have to do it within the parameters of two rules for successful first conversations.

Within the first 3–5 seconds after saying hello, your target is going to make a decision. He or she is going to be thinking... *"Is this person worth listening to or not? Is this person someone who is wasting my time or someone who may have something that is beneficial to me?"* Within the first 3 – 5 seconds of your target's saying hello, you must plant the impression that it would be beneficial to listen to you just a bit longer.

If targets do not have that mindset (assuming that you are speaking to someone who has a need that you can fill and would be willing to act) it really doesn't matter what you say after that because their mind has shut down. They have made an initial judgment that you are not worthwhile.

I really do believe that once their minds shut down, you could tell them that you want to show up to their office with $500 cash as a gift with no strings attached and they would still turn you down. When they don't perceive you as someone who is worthwhile, nothing you say has any impact on them.

Notice also that I phrased what you had to do in the first 3–5 seconds based upon the assumption that you were talking to someone who had a need that you could fill and who would be willing to act. Those are the people you are seeking to influence. You must give those people the information they need that will lead them to conclude they should talk with you or meet with you or get a quote from you. And, you need to get them to this conclusion within 3-5 seconds from their "hello."

If they do not have a need you can fill or they would not be willing to act, then what they think about you is irrelevant. Focus on making an initial connection (with those who have a need you can fill) within seconds of when targets pick up the phone.

So, let's dissect the script and let me use the second meeting script as an example.

The opening is: *"My name is Pauline Prospector from Super Service Group. We specialize in helping companies select widgets, wadgets and gizmos that best meet their needs. Companies like L. L. Beanstock, Enginola, and I. B. Sorry use us because we are experts and our prices are very competitive."*

What have we done within seconds of getting our decision-maker on the phone? We've identified who we are and where we are calling from. We have told them, point blank and very directly, what it is we do. *"We specialize in helping companies select widgets, wadgets and gizmos that best meet their needs."*

We have absolutely slayed them with a credibility statement that communicates we are not small time nor are we fly by nights. We have delivered a statement that communicates credibility unquestionably. When you drop names like L. L. Beanstock, Enginola, and I. B. Sorry you instantly communicate that you are a major player... that you are knowledgeable and that you are credible.

Now, if you have connected with someone who has a need for widgets, wadgets or gizmos, you have told them within seconds that this is what you do. They don't have to guess now about what you do. You have communicated unquestionably that you are a substantial player in this industry because you dropped three names of companies that would not do business with anyone less than a top shelf player.

Within seconds of "hello"... if that person on the other end of the line has a need... let me say again — if that person on the other end of the line has a need, you have given him/her cause for pause.

You have planted the thought that, *"Hey, maybe I should listen a bit longer. I have those specs on my desk now or that order is coming up in a few months...* " The target might also start to think about other issues like: *"My current vendor is a bit shaky and I am not really happy with the level of service I am getting."* Or: *"Hmmm, they help companies select widgets, wadgets and gizmos... and they must know what they are doing or they wouldn't have clients like L. L. Beanstock, Enginola and I. B. Sorry. I will listen a bit longer because there might be something in it for me."* Or even: *"They might make my job easier... do a better job than my current vendors... save me some money."*

That is what you need to happen within seconds of connecting with someone who has a need that you can fill.

Now a couple of observations here. First of all, understand that people think 10 times faster than they can speak or listen. So, in addition to people listening to what you say, there is an avalanche of thoughts going through their heads and you want them to be positive.

You can't give them time to think on their own. The natural tendency of the situation is for people to jump to the conclusion... that you are an idiot... that you don't have what they need... that you are bothering them... that you seem nice but they nevertheless want to get you off the phone as soon as possible so that they can get back to what they are doing before you called.

Notice what I did **not** recommend that you do in these first few seconds. (I know that these next few comments are going to rub a few people the wrong way. They always do.)

Notice that I did not say *"Hi how are you today? This is Pauline Perky or Charlie Chatty from Super Service group and I was wondering if you have few moments? Is this a good time to talk?"*

First of all, nobody cares. You don't care about how they are doing and they know you don't care about how they are doing today. So any such drivel wastes precious seconds.

It also gives them time to conclude that you are like all the other telemarketers who waste their time. And why shouldn't they conclude that? They get a lot of calls. Most of them are from amateurs and the vast majority of them are a bothersome waste of their time.

My strong feeling on this subject is based on experience. I know that many people feel more comfortable with the social chit chat on the first contact. But, I have never seen it work on the initial phone call. I, too, would feel more comfortable if it did. Naturally, I would prefer to have a comfortable, relaxed conversation with a prospect on the phone. I personally wish that the *"Hi, how are you... is this a bad time... have you got a few minutes"* type of banter would work. If it did, I would use it. But it doesn't.

If you are able to generate all the new accounts you need and hit your numbers and produce to your full potential with that type of opening line to a total stranger on the phone, I would say that is great. Good for you. Hurrah! But, I do not want to be at all wishy-washy on this matter. I have not seen the friendly chat-chat opener work that way.

Let's look at it another way. The people you are targeting are top executives making fairly large economic decisions. These are decisions that have far more impact than just the price of what they are purchasing. They are busy. You would have to assume that the kind of person who is going to buy enough product or services to make you a lot of money is a busy person. So, <u>why give</u>

So what have you done with your "Hi, how are you... is this a good time... do you have a few minutes" banter in those first precious seconds of your conversation? You have given them the time to conclude they should get rid of you. And, you have given them no reason to conclude that it may be in their best interest to listen to you a bit further.

them the opportunity to say they are busy and terminate the call before you tell them what you can do and just how credible you are?

Much of the work I have done for clients has been for companies that are making major sales... minimum of a quarter million dollars and up. People who make those types of decisions are very busy. The people we're trying to communicate with are difficult to reach. They don't know us. They don't know what we do. And, they don't know just how good we are nor how we can prove it until we tell them.

Until that information is provided, these busy decision makers have no reason to conclude that we are worth even a few seconds of their time... that we are better than anyone else who calls... that we are credible... that we can help them. They don't know until we tell them!

Also, let's also be very direct about something. We are interrupting them. If someone has no need that we can fill, or is perfectly happy with their current supplier, they can say, "I am not interested and have no time for this" once they know what we can do and how credible we are.

But, the people who have no need that we can fill are not my concern. I don't care about them. I care only about connecting with the decision makers who have a need that we can fill. I only care about communicating to those decision makers what we can do and just how credible we are, so that they have enough information to quickly conclude that they should listen to me a bit longer. If I don't give them that information, they cannot reach that conclusion. Simple!

We have to interrupt their train of thought and pull them away from whatever else they are doing when we call. We want to get them to focus on us for a moment rather than what they were doing when they picked up the phone. So, it is an interruption to launch immediately into your spiel when they pick up the phone, but I believe that you have no choice.

There are certain things you have to communicate within seconds or you will lose those who do have a need you can fill. Enough said.

So we start out. Your prospect says "Hello." And our script begins "This is Charlie Chatty from Super Service Group. We specialize in helping companies acquire widgets, wadgets and gizmos that best meet their needs. Companies like L. L. Beanstock, Enginola, and I. B. Sorry use us because we are experts and our prices are very competitive."

Now we continue with the rest of the script. At this point, my personal preference is to change the pace and tone of the script. So, where (in the first few seconds) I am very direct and straightforward, now as I get to second number ten or so, I adopt a different tone.

The script would continue like this. *"I have no idea if you might be looking for information or options regarding technology equipment. If you are, we would like the opportunity to introduce ourselves to you... give you some information and strategies companies have used to reduce delivery times and cut costs. If you hear something you like and think of us in the future that would be great. Would you have any time in the next week or two?"*

Boom . End of script! Now you do the hardest thing in the world for a salesperson to do. You shut up and listen.

Let's dissect it. *"I have no idea if you might be looking for information or options regarding your technology equipment."* With that sentence, we have changed the tone to be a bit more laid back and we now use language that is very open ended.

We don't know anything about the needs of who we are calling, so we use very broad general terms like "information" or "options" or "strategies." I have discovered that people love strategies. So, try to work that into your scripts whenever you can.

We also tell them again (in a general way) what we do so that there is no doubt in their mind. *"looking for information or options regarding technology equipment."*

So what we have done with the middle of the script is to change the tone a bit and admit the obvious. We have no idea whether they are "looking"… we have phrased things in a very general way… "information" or "options"…. that doesn't eliminate much … but… "regarding your technology equipment" clarifies what we do so that there is no confusion.

That is a lot for one sentence to do but this structure does it well. So, we have told them (in about 18 seconds) who we are and where we are calling from and what we do. We've also underscored why we are so credible. Then, we oriented their thinking to where we need it to be. Are they looking for information or options regarding their purchase of technology equipment?

With the last statement of our script, we tell them specifically, clearly and unequivocally exactly what it is we want them to do. *"If you are, we would like the opportunity to introduce ourselves, give you information on some programs that other companies have found valuable. If you hear something you like and think of us in the future, that would be great. Would you have any time in the next week or two?"* Boom! End of script.

Notice that we are accomplishing a number of things with that last line. We are asking for the opportunity to introduce ourselves. That goes down a lot easier and is a lot softer than saying we want to meet with you to try to sell you something. That statement does not create any resistance from our target. Essentially all we're saying is that "we want to give you some information on things we do differently and some programs that other companies have found valuable."

What have we conveyed? We are going to give them information on things that other companies have found valuable.

Maybe we have something they could benefit from. Other companies have benefited. Maybe they will.

The sentence continues... *"If you hear something you like and think of us in the future that would be great. Would you have any time in the next week or two."* What we are doing with that statement is taking away all the pressure and deflating resistance to a meeting. We talk about introducing ourselves… about giving them information on valuable programs… and we've told them that if they think of us in the future that would be great.

We are communicating to them that we are not going to push them to sign a purchase order at this meeting. We're telling them that we are not going to pressure them. Then we ask them very directly what it is we need to know. Do they have any time in the next week or two?

The voicemail script.

The intent of a voicemail message is not for people to actually return your calls. Very few will. The purpose is to act as a commercial that works in conjunction with your faxes to increase name recognition and increase their recognition of exactly what it is that Super Service Group does.

Very simply, voicemail is a "touch" and the more touches we have with a prospect with consistent, concise, direct benefit-rich messages, the more likely it is that they will recognize who we are and what we might do for them.

If that happens, it greatly increases the chance they will respond to a fax or a voicemail message, be more receptive to your phone call or call you when they have a need. That is why we leave voicemail messages. It is part of a total strategy to penetrate the minds of our prospects.

SAMPLE SET THE APPOINTMENT SCRIPT
AD SALES

Hi, this is _____ from _____. We have a collection of commercials that have been run successfully by insurance agencies nationwide... along with many scripts and promotional ideas that have worked in your industry... I would like to share this information with you and provide some options and strategies as to how radio may fit into your marketing mix. I know you will pick up a few good ideas and hope you think of us in the future. Would you have some time in the next week or two?

SAMPLE SET THE APPOINTMENT SCRIPT
DATA WAREHOUSING

Hi, this is Pat Prospector from ABC Corp. We help companies running Oracle, Sequel or DB2 with database diagnostics, monitoring and application development. Companies like No Capital, BA&A and Horizon have selected us to relieve their DBA staffing burden and improve their database performance. I don't know what your needs are, but would like to introduce ourselves and provide you with some options and strategies that have worked for others. Would you have some time in the next week or two?

Here is the script: *"If you are looking to replace widgets, wadgets or gizmos, companies like L. L. Beanstock, Enginola and I. B. Sorry use us to select and install systems that best meet their needs. If you are looking for information or a quote, we can help. This is Charlie Chatty from Super Service Group 1-800-123-4567 extension 1234."*

This is a 20-second script. Look at all that you do in 20 seconds. *"If you are looking to replace widgets, wadgets or gizmos..."* In the first 3 seconds of your message you have just told them simply and directly what it is you do. If they have a need, they will hopefully listen for a few more seconds before deleting you.

Then you continue "companies like L. L. Beanstock, Enginola and I. B. Sorry use us." Look at what has happened here within six seconds. If someone who has a need you can fill is listening, they know (without doubt) what you do and that you might be able to fill a need they have. Not only that... you have slayed them by dropping three recognizable names that communicate you are a major player and someone with credibility in the industry.

Now, if they have a need you can fill, they know that and they know you are credible... all done within 7 seconds. Now you continue... *"L. L. Beanstock, Enginola and I. B. Sorry use us to select and install systems that best meet their needs. If you are looking for information or options we can help. This is Charlie Chatty from Super Service group 800-123-4567 extension 1234."*

When we finish up, we ask a broad question... "If you are looking for information or options, we can help." Now finally at the end, we tell them who we, where we're from and our phone number.

What is unusual about this script? You don't identify yourself or leave your number until the very end. Why? Let's think about it. If someone who has a need we can fill is listening to us, the probability is that as soon as we identify ourselves as a tele-marketer we'll get deleted. That's because most telemarketers waste the time of decision makers.

But, if we structure the script as I've shown, we'll have their attention within the first 3 seconds. And, within the first 7 sec-onds, we will have conveyed credibility. So, <u>if they have a need we can fill,</u> we have a real shot of their at least listening to the message.

Now, of course, if they are not a person who has a need we can fill, they will also know that within seconds and will delete our message. So what!?

SAMPLE VOICEMAIL SCRIPT
DATA WAREHOUSING

If improving database performance or reducing DBA staffing costs would benefit you, companies like Mega Industries, Microhard and Horizon have selected us to improve their reliability and save money. If you would like some information on options this is Super Salesperson from 123Corp. 978-123-4567.

SAMPLE VOICEMAIL SCRIPT
SALES TRAINING

If setting more sales appointments with high level decision makers at targeted accounts would improve your sales productivity, you can receive a free tutorial of strategies and a sample audio CD of proven methods. Contact me directly at 978-927-5099 or check out findingbusiness.com. This is Scott Channell of Finding Business. 978-927-5099.

6

Responding To Objections: Six Concepts You Must Understand

Working within these concepts separates the wimps from the appointment setters

You must understand and appreciate six concepts to effectively respond to objections.

1. THEY EXPECT TO SAY "NO"

Every molecule in your suspect's body is aching to say the word "no."

They don't have time. They have no need. They have had too much time wasted before by teleprospector's who called in the past. So, they say "no." Your targets' immediate thought when they realize they are being prospected is to think, *"I am not going to do this."*

They have been on the receiving end of many of these calls before and know the drill. It is the natural pattern.

For you to get them to consider a "yes" you must get them out of familiar territory.

If you act and sound like most of the callers who preceded you, what do you expect the result to be?

The result will be the same. "No Thanks."

Be different from previous callers. Use words that are more powerful than their normal natural knee-jerk "no" reaction.

2. YOU DON'T HEAR "OBJECTIONS"

When prospecting, we want to effectively overcome "objections." But, let me ask you this question. Do you think it is *really* accurate to think of what we seek to overcome as "objections?"

Let me explain. I think that for something to be accurately labeled an "objection," it has to be based upon some knowledge or some modicum of understanding and appreciation of what is being presented before it can truly and meaningfully be "objected" to.

Is that really what is happening when we are prospecting? It might be more appropriate to entitle this section "overcoming resistance." It is natural for our targets to resist efforts to schedule a meeting with them. They resist our efforts by speaking words that sound very similar to someone who is actually raising an "objection."

Although the words sound the same, they are substantively different. And, because they are substantively different, your response to them has to also be different in order to achieve the primary purpose of your phone call.

Example.

When a salesperson goes out to meet a prospect multiple times (listening carefully) and probably also has a few phone calls with that prospect, he/she usually earns the opportunity to present a quote or a proposal. But then, in the final stage of the deal, the prospect starts discussing reasons why the salesperson's company may not get the order. Those are "**Objections!**"

Sometimes, the prospect has been meaningfully informed about what you can do but still expresses reservations or rejects moving forward.

Those are objections in the truest sense of the word. A salesperson, at that stage of the sales process, must truly *overcome* the objection and fully satisfy the prospect. In order to close the deal, the salesperson has to make the prospect comfortable. In order to do that the salesperson has to respond fully and completely and leave nothing out.

But when we are prospecting, our objective is not to close a deal. It is to schedule a sales appointment with a decision-maker at a qualified company. When we are prospecting, we are not overcoming objections as much as we are responding to resistance. And, when seeking to schedule a sales appointment while responding to the suspect's natural resistance, what we purposely leave **unsaid** is just as important in achieving our objective as what we choose to verbalize.

At the closing stage of the sales process, if we don't fully satisfy prospects and give them all the information they request, the deal does not get closed. But, when prospecting, if we fully answer all the prospect's questions and give them all the information they request, there is no longer a reason for them to meet with us. In other words, we will have prematurely knocked ourselves out of the sales appointment setting game.

3. PROMISE THEM BENEFITS *AT THE FIRST MEETING*

Remember that the number one reason prospects don't agree to meet with us is because we don't give them enough reason to meet with us. The reasons that prospects should meet with us have to be delivered at the very first meeting.

So, when you engage your prospect in a conversation, you have to always keep in mind that in order to achieve the purpose of your call, any additional conversation is an opportunity for you to reinforce the benefits they will receive at the first meeting.

Think about those "set-the-meeting" scripts that have been developed and used effectively to date. Although the words may differ, the format of the winning scripts are essentially the same. You tell people who you are... where you are calling from... and what you do. You build credibility by dropping names of well known clients. Then you relate the benefits that companies get by working with you. You might mention: expertise, quick response, competitive pricing or some things that you do differently that other companies have found helpful. This is, likewise, the time to mention the unique programs you offer. You also mention that you can provide them with information, options and strategies. Those are the benefits people will get by agreeing to meet with you.

You then end up by telling them exactly what you want them to do and asking them for the meeting. This is the successful formula for scoring a meeting. Prospects can say yes... they can say no... or, they can offer some resistance you must respond to.

When prospects offer some resistance you should consider this as an opportunity to provide them with additional benefits or re-affirm the benefits they will get at the meeting and once again ask for the meeting.

No matter where prospects want to go with the conversation, you'll always want to steer it back to your original purpose by restating the benefits they get by spending time with you and again asking for a meeting.

4. NEVER LOSE CONTROL

You must always maintain control over the conversation. If you lose control over the conversation, you are going to get caught in "Maybe Land."

Once you lose control over the conversation or let it drift away from your agenda (which is to book a meeting) you can only lose in another more important way.

How do you lose? Once you lose control of the conversation, you'll be thrust into that "send me information... call me back... hey, why don't you spend time to put together a quote or proposal for me (even though the odds are high I won't purchase from you)" dimension. And that, my friend, is a very low productivity place to be in.

We have previously touched upon the necessity of thinking in terms of *groups*. Rather than caring about what happens on any individual call or whether you penetrate any individual account, worry much more about how effective you are with a whole group of prospects. Consider the following as a good example of why you have to think in terms of groups.

If you concentrate on individuals, once they start talking about their standards... their issues... their challenges, or what-ever else they bring up, your natural tendency will be to think: *"Well this is important to them. I know a lot about that. I'll show them how smart I am and tell them the most important things right now."*

But if you do that, you are actually making a couple of strategic errors. First, remember that gravity is working against you. Your targets **expect** to decline your request for a meeting. The more you talk, the more opportunity you give them to conclude that a meeting would not be worth their time. Second, if you answer their questions, they don't need you anymore. So why meet?

And third, when you respond in detail to what they say, you are now working on *their* agenda and you have abandoned your own agenda.

If any of those three things happen: you talk too much; you give out too much information; or you let them determine the course of the conversation, you can only lose.

You lose because almost always the result of the conversation will be to pitch head long into "Maybe Land." By your decisions and your actions, you have slotted those records into a group in which you know there is a low probability of success.

You want to be able to slot them into a group in which there is a much higher probability of success. And that group is the group that has agreed to meet with you. You'll always maximize the odds for scheduling a meeting if you maintain control of the conversation and always come back to your agenda.

One other aside on the topic of maintaining control of the conversation should be considered here. Most successful conversations last about 2 ½ to 3 minutes. It is my personal opinion that you have to try to steer the conversation to a successful conclusion within that 2 ½ to 3 minutes. If the conversation goes on longer than that, the odds decrease that someone will book a meeting with you.

This will happen when you either give them the most valuable information or don't give them *enough* reason to meet with you. The longer you talk, the more opportunity you give prospects to hang their hat on something that will lead them to conclude, "*It's not worth my time to meet with this person.*"

Remember: they are *expecting* to conclude that it is not worth their time to meet with you. If you speak too long, you make it a whole lot easier for them to reach that conclusion.

5. EVERY WORD COUNTS

You must ruthlessly eliminate unnecessary or wishy-washy words. You have a very short period of time and you are fighting gravity. Any word that is not directly reinforcing why targets should meet with you and what they will get from that meeting should be eliminated. Eliminate general meaningless – waste of breath – just fill up space type phrases.

What are they? They are statements like: *"We want to see what we can do for you." "We want to tell you about the services we offer" or "We want to see if there is anything we can do to help you."* Anything you say that is non-specific and not related to communicating a **benefit** they will <u>get at that first meeting</u> should be eliminated.

Once you have given it your best shot, you are better off to be silent than to fill space with wishy-washy, meaningless words.

Tip: Tape record your end of the conversation. Place a tape recorder on your desk set on record pause. When a decision maker says "Hello," start recording. You will hear all the unnecessary words and pauses that slip into your conversation. Eliminate them. You will also hear what you sound like to your targets. You can alter your words, tone and delivery to maximize results.

6. BE RELAXED AND CONFIDENT

It is not only what you say but how you say it that counts. You want to be projecting a relaxed and confident demeanor. You are calling from a great company with a long list of good clients. You are providing high quality products and services. It is the most natural and normal thing in the world for you to be calling companies and seeking a meeting. And… it would be the most normal, natural thing in the world for them to agree to do so.

When you think and plan out in advance what words you will use to achieve your objective and then you deliver those words naturally and confidently (without hemming or hawing and without hesitations... without uh uh uh... without throwing in needless and meaningless words), you greatly increase the odds that people will conclude that it will be worth spending time with you.

When you seem to be searching for words or hesitating and not quite sure of yourself on the phone, what do you think is going through your prospect's mind? I'd guess they'll probably think something like this: "Well if this person isn't quite sure of what to say over the phone, how worthwhile would it be for me to have a meeting with them?"

7
Responding To Resistance

You hear the same objections repeatedly.
There is no excuse for not handling them well.

You want to now think out in advance the best way to respond to resistance you will encounter.

This is important for two reasons.

First, 25% to 40% of the meetings you schedule will be booked in the same conversation that started with a "no" to your initial request.

When your first request for a meeting is denied, you are now at the moment of truth. These are the skills that separate effective appointment setters (and subsequently quota busting salespeople) from those who are left muttering excuses and thinking "what if... ?"

If you are not prepared you will lose those opportunities and all your efforts to position yourself to have those conversations will be wasted.

You must leverage your target's response, re-state the benefits they will get at the first meeting, *then again ask for the meeting.*

Second, many future opportunities are identified when you respond effectively to resistance. If you don't respond effectively, you will not identify those future opportunities.

In fact, after you have been using these strategies for 2–3 months, you can expect that 33% to 50% of your meetings will be scheduled with people who told you when to follow-up with them and gave their permission and encouragement to do so.

It is your effective response to resistance strategies that elicit that information.

COMMON SCENARIOS

There are really only about a half dozen common scenarios you have to prepare for. When you recognize them, it will seem like a big giant melon has been pitched to you right over the plate and you are going to smash it right out of the park.

The seven common forms of resistance you will encounter over the phone are as follows:

1. I'm all set.

2. Send some info.

3. Call me back.

4. Tell me.

5. We are not buying right now.

6. I get 20 calls a day from people like you

7. I'll meet with you but call me in a month.

Before we go into specifically how you might best respond to these situations, one final comment.

When you are prospecting, the bigger picture is that you are trying to re-shuffle the deck in order of priorities. You identify your very best opportunities and schedule appointments with them. You identify your no-opportunity or low probability targets and get rid of them. In the middle you have various shades of gray you have to sort in some order of priority.

You obtain much of the information you need to sort suspects when you retain control and effectively respond to initial resistance.

Responding to "we are all set..."

This is sometimes expressed as "we have a vendor we love," "we have five vendors," or even "we have a contract with 22 years left to run which is unbreakable."

Here are two options for how to reply:

"That's fine. Does that mean you are never going to look at new options or could you suggest a better time for me to call in the future?"

Or

"That's fine. Look, we wouldn't expect anything to happen quickly anyway. That's not the way it happens in this business. We do an awful lot of business with companies like Mega Corp, International Amalgamated and Acme Intergalactic and there are good reasons why companies like these decided to work with us. We would just be looking for the opportunity to introduce ourselves and give you some information on programs and strategies to make your process a bit easier. And, if in the future you are looking for options or need a hard-to-source item, we hope you would think of us. Would that be worth 30 minutes of your time in the next few weeks?"

Now with the first response, "*That's fine. Does that mean you are never going to look at new options or could you suggest a better time for me to call you in the future?*" What you are doing is giving your prospect the opportunity to reconfirm what they just told you and give you permission as well as direction for when to call again. You have no chance of getting a meeting with this response since you haven't given additional reasons for why they should meet with you and you haven't asked for a meeting again. So, this response is probably best when you have someone who is very gruff or who appears rushed and you don't feel you can give the longer response.

It is very important that you ask them when to call back. It never ceases to amaze me how people in one breath tell you emphatically they have no need, yet in the next breath will tell you they will be buying in 30 days. This happens frequently.

If you humbly accept the "no," you won't identify the great opportunities that are lurking just beneath the surface of that answer.

Another option to use. *"That's fine. I don't want to be on your back, but we do an awful lot of this. Could you suggest a time I should call in the future?"*

If they truly have no need, they will reconfirm that. But, if they are open to listening to some options at some point, you have done something calculated to discover that fact.

My personal opinion is that you should try some variation of the longer response.

"That's fine. Look, we wouldn't expect anything to happen quickly anyway. That's not the way it happens in this business. We do an awful lot of business with companies like Mega Corp, International Amalgamated and Acme Intergalactic and they selected us because they save time, administrative headaches and costs. We would just be looking to introduce ourselves and give

you some information on programs and strategies to make your process a bit easier. If in the future you are looking for options, we would hope you think of us. Would that be worth 30 minutes of your time in the next few weeks?"

What you are doing with this script is lowering their expectations and reassuring them that you are not asking them to change. You then re-establish your credibility by mentioning how much business you do and dropping the names of more great companies that have chosen to do business with you.

Notice the terms *"other companies have chosen us"* and *"expertise."* These are the little things you drop to convey benefits and to convince someone it would be worth their time to meet with you. Then you end up by telling them what they will get <u>at that meeting</u>, not in the future, but <u>at that meeting</u>.

You continue with, *"We will give you some information on X Y and Z and some strategies to make your process a bit easier."*

You then go for the close by saying " If in the future you are looking for options or need to source a hard-to-find item, we hope you think of us. Would that be worth 30 minutes of your time?"

Or your final line can be, "If that is worth 30 minutes of your time, would you be available on April 1st or 2nd?"

If you feel comfortable with it, the second question, *"If that is worth 30 minutes of your time, would you be available on April 1st or 2nd?"* is better because they need to say yes only once.

So what you have done is kept control of the conversation; given them additional reasons to meet with you and asked for the meeting. If they say no, you then ask them to suggest a good time for you to call them back.

Responding to *"send me some information."*
(Are you a wimp or an appointment setter?)

This is probably the most common thing you will hear. Let me be blunt. If your response to "*Send me some information*" is "*um OK,*" you are a wimp and you are dooming yourself to prospecting frustration. You're also wasting a lot of time and company resources.

We know that most of the time when someone says "Send me some information," it is really a blow-off. Rather than tell you to get lost, they mumble a request to send them something and for them the phone call is over.

But (as you know) if you let the caller control the call, you lose. Because then you will have doomed yourself to calling back... calling back... banging your head against the wall and getting frustrated because people who asked for information (who you thought might have a legitimate need) don't return your calls. When, after 10 or 15 attempts, if you do get them back on the phone, almost always they at best vaguely remember you. If they did get something you sent they haven't read it or they can't remember receiving it. Almost always, the end of the road is a "No."

If you just say "ok" to the send-more-information-blow-off, you have received no information of value to your prospecting efforts.

If you get on this treadmill, it is <u>your own fault,</u> not the fault of the people you are targeting. Remember that your objective in prospecting is not just to set sales appointments, it is to re-shuffle the deck and sort your prospects in accordance with their potential value and worth.

Not only that, the people who are legitimately high-potential, high-value prospects are not given the opportunity to identify themselves to you.

If you don't give those types of prospects the opportunity to identify themselves, you won't know who they are and you won't know who is worth more of your time.

The next time you get the send-more-information-blow-off, consider saying something like this:

"You know, I don't send out general information. The corporate literature I might send you is only going to tell you what I just told you. We are a $90 million dollar company that's been in business 15 years supplying technology equipment like widgets and wadgets to companies such as United Intergalactic, Mega Corp and I. B. Sorry Corp. If there is some specific information that would be helpful to you, or if you happen to have a specific purchase coming up, I would be happy to put together something specific to your needs and send it to you. Do you have anything specific in mind that I can help you with?"

And at that point… you do the most difficult thing a salesperson ever has to do. You say nothing and wait for your prospect to speak.

If he/she can't come up with something specific, recognize that you have delivered your most powerful benefit-laden credibility building message. If they don't respond with something specific so that you can properly prioritize them, you can with confidence go right into plan B.

If prospects do come up with something specific, like, *"Well, … we are going to replace $500,000 worth of widgets in a month…"* or *"well, we are going to buy $1,200,000 worth of stuff next quarter. Why don't you send me some info on x y or z?"* You'll now know you have "a live one" and you have to do three things.

First, you have to really listen. Let them speak. Don't interrupt. When they are done, ask a couple of open-ended questions to clarify their request and allow them to give you more information about their needs. And then, come back to your agenda.

Remember, we started out by saying that you never let your targets' agenda become your own agenda. They may be asking you for information, but you need a **meeting**. The odds of landing an account go up substantially when you get a face-to-face meeting.

So, when a target has told you he/she has a specific need or purchase coming up, it is even more important that you land a meeting. And remember: the most frequent reason people don't meet with us is that we don't give them enough reason to meet with us and we don't *ask* for a meeting.

So, after listening to their request and then clarifying it with a couple of open ended questions, you then swing the conversation back to *your* agenda and say something like the following.

"You know, I could put together a lot of info that would be useful to you...right off the top of my head I can think of three companies in your industry that we've helped to select and install what you seem to be looking for. I don't know a lot of details about your company. But, you do have a few options to consider on this and there are a couple of things you want to avoid that could really cost you some money. Super Salesperson is our rep in your area and she has a lot of experience with this. If she had the opportunity to learn more specifics about your company, she could give you a lot of information that would be helpful to you and specific to your situation. It may or may not lead to a next step... either is fine. I could set up a meeting for you now. Would that be worth 30 minutes of your time?"

Let's look at what you will have done. You will have given those companies that **do** have a specific need the opportunity to inform you of that need. And you will have leveraged that information into a tremendous benefit that they will receive if they agree to meet with you. They will get specific information on their particular needs from someone who is very knowledgeable. That is usually a pretty good reason for people to meet with you.

If they say "yes," book it. If they say "no," tell them you will send out the info and ask when you should follow up.

Now, before we get off the send-more-info-objection, I would like you to keep two other points in mind. First, remember that sometimes our greatest strength can be our greatest weakness. It is very difficult for someone who has a lot of knowledge in a particular area to withhold information when talking to a suspect. But that is exactly what you have to do at this stage of the process.

What you decide to withhold is as important as what you decide to say. If you provide too much information, you give suspects the opportunity to conclude that they should not meet with you. Every bone in their body is looking for a reason **not** to meet with you. And, when the conversation lasts more than 2 ½ or 3 minutes, you will probably give them something to hang their hat on as a justification for blowing you off.

Also, if you talk too much, you are talking about their agenda and not *your* agenda and you can only lose in that arena.

Likewise notice what did **not** happen during this conversation. As soon as you heard about a potential purchase, you did not did not fall into, "*Hey, what are your standards? Give me more specifics on your order. Let me run around and put together a quote for you.*" mode. Good! Do not do that.

As a group we know that when we just give a quote for an order to a company that we haven't met, we have only a very, very, slight chance of ever converting that into an account. When we meet with someone and then provide a quote, we have a 1 in 5 to a 1 in 8 chance of gaining an account.

If you have a live one, where would you like to work? With a 1 in 100 chance that it will become an account or with a 1 in 5 chance that it will become an account? If you drop into the "let me put a quote together for you mode too quickly," bear in mind that it is by _**your decision**_ and _**your actions**_ that at best you will have put yourself into the quote category when it might have been just as easy to slide into the meeting category.

Make every effort to schedule the meeting first. And, make sure targets tell you they absolutely don't want to schedule a meeting before you go to "Plan B" or seek a quote opportunity.

Responding to "Call me back..."

Let me give you some things to think about with this form of resistance. The majority of the time, this is just another blow-off and if you just say "ok," you'll be acting in accordance with **their agenda**. You lose. You'll soon know that you are doomed to making call after call only to get nowhere.

Once you have them on the phone, you need to get some information to properly slot them so that **you** can decide whether or not you will call them back.

I would recommend that you proceed as follows:

"_I would be happy to do that. When would you suggest I call you?_"

Once they give you a time period, say, "_I would be happy to contact you then. Is there a specific reason why that's a good time to call you?_"

They will then tell you, essentially, one of two things. They will give you a general "_I am really busy right now_" or "_There is nothing happening_" type response. On the other hand, they may give you a specific response with information that is helpful to your agenda of finding out whether you have a realistic chance of making a worthwhile sale or not.

That specific response will typically be something like, "*Well, we **are** planning to buy a billion dollars worth of product or services that you sell and I will have the specs then.*" Or, "*I know we are going to review our vendors and I would like to hear more about your company.*" Or, "*I'm in the middle of month-end; quarter-end; year-end and won't be able to focus on our needs in this area until then.*"

Once you get a valid, legitimate reason and know that you have a viable prospect, you can end up by saying:

"Thank you very much. I will contact you then. One quick question... How many employees do you have (or how many users do you have, or how many employee relocations do you do every year, or how many salespeople do you have?")

They give the reply and you end by saying "I'll talk to you in two months." Click.

Now, if they give you a very generic non-specific reason or *say, "I just don't have time for this right now.*" There is something you need to discover. Is this a run-me-around-the-block time-wasting; no need; go nowhere suspect who thinks I am just going to call, and call, and call on their whim? Is this someone who is going to suck every bit of motivation and energy out of my body by having me chase them and get nothing for my time and effort? Or... is this someone who legitimately would welcome a call from me for a legitimate reason at some point in the future?

You can find out now; or you can find out 10 phone calls from now. Your choice!

So, (if you have some guts) let's see if you could bring yourself to say something like this: "*I'd be happy to call you back... but keep in mind that we've provided companies like x, y and z about $100 million worth of widgets and wadgets and we are do-*

ing quite well. I don't want to be on your back. If you are not open to a new source of supply just tell me and I won't bother you. "

Or, *"I'd be happy to call you back. We've done projects with companies like X, Y and Z...(Or, you might say... "achieved results like ABC for many companies like yours.) I don't want to be on your back. If you don't think it would be worthwhile for me to call back, it is perfectly OK to say that."*

Now if you say something like that, they will probably respond with a reply like, *"Well, I really am not going to have anything for you."* To which you can say "Why don't I call you in six months? Thankyouverymuch." Click.

Or... they will say something to the effect *"Oh no! I want you to call me. We are (or will be) looking for your product/ service options."* To that reply you respond: *"That's great. I'll call you in two months. Thankyouverymuch."* Click.

Now let's look at what you have done with a few, simple, direct questions... asked with surgical precision.

In any group of 100 send-me-some-information responses, we know that 90 or more of them are blow-offs. At best 10 of them may lead to a legitimate opportunity. You have them on the phone now. Ask the questions and separate the time-wasters from the legitimate opportunities.

"Sure. I would be happy to call you back. Is there a specific reason why you want me to call you at that time?" Or: *"Oh! Well, I would be happy to call you. But look, we provide companies like x, y and z with about $100 million worth of technology equipment a year. I don't want to be on your back if you don't have a need or don't plan on looking at vendor options. Do you really think it would be worthwhile for me to call you in two months? It's perfectly OK for you to tell me if it won't be."*

My personal opinion is that it's a whole lot easier to learn how to get those few simple questions out and get the information you need than it is to be frustrated, de-motivated, and a lot poorer because you let people run you around the flagpole and waste your time.

Responding to the rest

Now, the balance of the most common forms of resistance are as follows:

- The tell me objection.
- The I get 20 calls a day like this objection.
- The home office is in Beirut objection.
- The I'll meet with you but call me in a month objection.

All the responses fall into a familiar pattern and we can cover them quickly.

First: the "I'll meet with you but call me in a month objection." Keep in mind that approximately half of those who specifically tell you they will meet with you but ask you to call back later **will** actually book a meeting with you. Half! And, that half usually only books after you get them on the phone again. No small achievement.

So, if their mindset is that they will meet with you, try to book a meeting now rather than later.

The conversation would go something like this. "*Sure, I would be happy to call you then. We would probably be looking to get together a few weeks after that. So... that would put us into the week of April 15th. We are in your area quite frequently and I know I could schedule a few other visits on the same trip. If you feel comfortable, would you mind if we penciled something in the week of April 15th or so? It would help me with my planning. I would call you a week before to make sure the time still works for you. Would you feel comfortable doing that?"*

Book it if they say yes - tell them you will call them in a month if they say no.

Now, on to the "tell me" objection which usually rears its head with words like "who are you?" or "what do you do?" Your best response is to tell them what you have already told them and again ask for the meeting.

Respond with: *"We work with companies like International Amalgamated, Acme Intergalactic and Humongous Corporation. They selected us to provide about $90 million worth of widgets and use us because they save time, administrative headaches and costs. We want to introduce ourselves and tell you about some things we do differently that other companies have found valuable. Our private inventory or maxi-marketplace programs may have some benefits for you and I'm asking for 30 minutes to give you that information. If you think of us in the future that would be great. Would you have some time in a few weeks say April 28 or 29th?"*

Don't delve into other areas or provide them with new information because all you'll do is give them too much to process and too much to think about. Remember: if there is any doubt in their mind, they will not agree to meet with you. Providing additional credibility statements and again telling them the benefits they would get at a meeting with you is the best course.

The "I get 20 calls a day like this" objection is a bit more complex. First of all, that objection only tells you that many teleprospectors (who are not as talented as you) have called this person before you. You also know that every bone and muscle in the body of your target is waiting to say no to you because that is the most common knee-jerk response to unsolicited calls.

You must fight gravity in this situation and immediately cut through all those pre-conceived notions your target has as to why he/she should deny your request.

Your response would be very similar to the "tell me" objection. *"Look, I don't want to be on your back. We are a $90 million company and other companies like A, B and C have selected us to source their widget equipment. I don't know yet if we might be able to help you. We do a few things differently that companies find save them time, administrative headaches and costs. We have a couple of unique programs like private inventory and maxi-marketplace that a lot of companies have found helpful. If getting info on strategies that have proven valuable to similar companies is worth 30 minutes of your time, that would be great. If not that's OK too. Would you have some time in the next week or two?"*

So what have you done? You re-established your credibility and told them about some powerful benefits they'll get if they meet with you. You also ignored their agenda, which is to moan about people calling them (a fact which is meaningless to us). You have kept the conversation on your agenda so that you get a clear "yes" or "no." That, then, freed you up so you can go onto your next call.

Also remember that just because a lot of people have called them already, it doesn't mean you don't have a shot at getting a meeting. Most telemarketers are pretty poor and you are much better than average so you can succeed where others fail.

The "the home office makes all the decisions and they are located in Beirut" objection is pretty straight forward. All you can really do is ask if they will tell you to whom you should send information in Beirut. Or, if they will tell you who is in charge of purchasing widget equipment. And then ask them if there is anyone at their site who has input into such decisions whom they would recommend you send some info to. They will either give you the names or they won't and you can decide to follow up or not.

So, again with your response, you establish credibility... tell them the benefits they will get if they agree to meet with you... and ask for the meeting.

Now most of the time (even if you are very good at setting sales appointments), in the real world most people will say no. That does not mean, however, that you cannot achieve an important purpose with your call.

We are prospecting — not simply appointment setting. One purpose of the call is to sort our suspects in order of priority. The suspects you talk to might have a need in the near future. The odds are certainly pretty good that, at some time in the future, they will buy from somebody. Virtually every company periodically re-evaluates their vendor relationships.

Prepare, practice and refine your response to common forms of resistance. Your response should be calculated to extract as much information as possible. In particular, you want to identify every future opportunity so that you can decide how best to follow up.

You want to be very direct with your response to resistance. You may initially feel uncomfortable asking such direct questions when someone has already told you they are not interested... get over it.

That initial discomfort is a small price to pay for filling up your sales pipeline with quality opportunities.

A NOTE ABOUT THE SAMPLE SCRIPTS IN THIS BOOK.

This book uses sample scripts from a couple different industries. I have tried to mix up the samples between product and service/consulting companies to demonstrate the winning formats. You should be able to recognize the winning structure in these scripts to create scripts specific to your situation.

If you would like help crafting the best scripts/ responses to resistance for your situation, contact me. There are a number of products/personal coaching/training options that can assist you.

Scott Channell
Finding Business
39 Dodge St. #288
Beverly MA 01915
978-927-5099 Fax 978-964-0199

www.settingsalesappointments.com
scottc@findingbusiness.com

SAMPLE RESPONSES TO RESISTANCE
MEDIA ADVERTISING COMPANY

Responding to "We are all set"

a. *"That's fine. Does that mean you are never going to look at new options or could you suggest a better time to call in the future?"*

b. *"That's fine. We wouldn't expect anything to happen quickly anyway. That's not the way it works in this business. We do an awful lot of business with companies like X, Y and Z, and there are good reasons why companies like that advertise with us. We would just be looking to introduce ourselves, give you some information on marketing options and strategies that have worked for others and hope you might think of us in the future. Would that be worth 30 minutes of your time during the next couple of weeks?"*

Responding to "Send some information" or "Send your rates"

"You know, we don't send out general information. The general corporate stuff I might send you is just going to tell you what I just told you...companies like X, Y and Z have found it beneficial to advertise with us and we have a large database of sample commercials, scripts and promotion ideas for the _____ industry that we would be happy to share. If you have a need for something specific... if you have a campaign or event coming up... I would be happy to take the time to put something specific together that might really help you. Do you have anything specific in mind that I can help you with?"

If they do...

"You know.. I could put together a lot of information that would be helpful... I can think of 3 companies we helped that had a simi-

lar problem... I don't have a lot of information on your company but you have a couple of options to consider and there are a couple of mistakes you want to avoid that would really cost you some money. If I had the opportunity to learn more about your company I could put something together specific to your needs... that may or may not lead to a next step.. either is fine.... Would that be worth 30 minutes of your time?"

Responding to "Call me back"

"I would be happy to do that, when would you suggest I call you?"

If they suggest a date...

"I would be happy to call then. Is there a specific reason why that is a good time to call you?"

If they don't suggest a date or provide a reason...

"You know.. I would be happy to call you back... companies like X, Y and Z use us and we have good information on how radio has produced results in your industry. I don't want to be on your back. If you don't want to consider radio as part of your marketing mix, just tell me... I won't bother you."

Responding to "Call me back to schedule a meeting"

"Sure, I would be happy to do that. That would put us into the week of _____. If you feel comfortable, do you mind if we pencil something in... it would help with my scheduling... I will call you the week before to make sure the time we set still works... would you feel comfortable doing that?"

Responding to " We only do newspapers and yellow pages."

"That's fine... many of our current advertisers felt the same way...companies like X, Y and Z have found that radio is an important part of their marketing mix and renew their schedules again and again...I would be happy to share some information and strategies as to how radio can supplement and work well with your other media... you'll definitely get a few good ideas and maybe you'll call us sometime in the future. Would that be worth 30 minutes sometime in the next few weeks."

Responding to "I tried it, it doesn't work" or "It's too expensive."

"Well, any marketing tool used improperly is guaranteed to not work... and local companies like X, Y and Z have found how to work radio into their marketing mix and keep renewing their schedules... there are reasons for that. Don't know what you did before... but I would be happy to provide you some information and strategies that have worked for businesses like yours...you'll probably learn a couple things and maybe you will call us in the future. Would that be worth 30 minutes of your time during the next couple of weeks?"

8

Plan "B"... Where Most Of The Economic Value Of Sales Prospecting Is To Be Found

Multiply your profits

Plan "B"... What is it and why is having one properly imple-mented so critical to capturing the highest return on your sales prospecting and appointment-setting efforts?

It is important because of these realities:

1. Most of the decision-makers you speak to will not agree to an immediate meeting.

2. Most of the target companies you prospect do not have an immediate need.

3. With "major sales" the odds of initially contacting someone at exactly the right time is low.

4. A good number of your targets are excellent short term (1-3 months) targets. They must be identified and nurtured cost effectively.

5. Many, many more of your targets are excellent longer term prospects (3 - 12 months). They also must be identified and nurtured cost effectively.

6. Most costs are up front. Most of the profits are in that group that doesn't immediately agree to meet.

7. Most prospects know what they want. Most, however, don't know what they *need*.

8. Many suspects you speak to, who have needs you could fill, will not disclose that to you because you have no credibility in their eyes. Your plan B strategy delivers that credibility and positions you for access at a future date.

9. The best prospects call you.

The sales prospecting program you establish MUST justify itself economically over the short term. This means that enough meetings get booked and convert to sales of sufficient size and profit margin within a reasonable time period to justify the time and money invested.

Thirteen long years ago, in the early days of my doing this, that was as far as my thinking went. All I thought about was booking meetings that resulted in closed deals and the program was a success. Nothing more.

Not much thought was given to a "phase II." I had no plan for how to get more from those who wouldn't immediately agree to a meeting or couldn't be reached on the phone.

But as I set up more and more successful programs, I came to realize that IN ADDITION TO the short term economic realities that must be met, THAT THERE WAS A FAR GREATER ECO-NOMIC BENEFIT TO BE GAINED FROM THOSE WHO WERE NOT RESPONSIVE DURING THE FIRST PASS.

When you are making a "major sale" (which I define as a sale that involves a large amount of money or great risk to the buying organization and typically involves a 3 to 18 month sales cycle), the odds of getting the right decision maker on the phone at the right time in that sales cycle and then getting an appointment with the first contact is not high.

Now again, let me emphasize that the instances in which this does happen must be sufficient for the program to justify itself in the start-up phase.

WHY YOU NEED A "PLAN B."

Even in wildly successful programs, most prospects will decline your request to meet with them. A rough rule of thumb that I use is that you can expect to book a meeting with one out of every six decision makers you speak to. Five of six will decline. There usually is a lot of great potential business among those five. If you don't have a solid "plan B," you won't have a chance to get that business.

You need a "plan B" to automatically follow up with viable prospects cost effectively and without your having to make numerous phone calls in the hopes that you catch them at the right time.

Most of your costs are up front and most of your profits are in that group of prospects that don't immediately agree to meet with you. Plan B enables you to realize a high return on investment from your prospecting activities since you will be able to generate business from those who don't immediately agree to meet. You do this by enabling them to "raise their hands" from the crowd when they are ready to buy.

"Plan B" gets them into your sales funnel and greatly increases:

1) The chance that they will contact you when they have a need. And,

2) That you will have the credibility to close a deal because they have been touched by you consistently over a period of time.

Most people know what they want; fewer know what they need. Plan B enables you to educate people about new options that will help them... options they had not previously been willing to consider. I have seen a lot of business generated as a result of effective plan B strategies from prospects whose response to an initial offer was a resounding "NO."

The very best prospects are those that call you. If you want people to call you, you have to include an effective plan B strategy into your prospecting program. After about three months of implementing these strategies about 25%-30% of your results will come from those who call you to initiate a relationship.

Why is it that someone would call you? Very simply because you have credibility in their eyes.

Credibility usually is earned with a consistent message over a period of time. Consistency builds credibility. With a consistent message over a period of time, your targets develop confidence that you have knowledge or expertise that can benefit them. They develop confidence that you have solved problems similar to theirs for others. They develop confidence that you may be able to help them, too.

COMPONENTS OF YOUR "PLAN B"

Always have some things to offer your targets THAT THEY WOULD GENUINELY VALUE AND DESIRE. They don't want info about your company. Even if they say they do I'd bet that they are either lying or delirious.

These offers that you think will be valuable to targets should account for the fact that your targets will be at varying stages of the sales process. Those in the very early stages of a long sales cycle (the just noodling around stage) will more likely respond to a different offer than those who will buy within 90 days.

The bottom line is that your system must identify these eager prospects out of the crowd. You must get them to "raise their hands" so that you can see them.

Your Plan B should anticipate sending multiple touches to targets on an automatic basis or as part of a group communication. If you think sending your company brochure to someone who has made pleasant sounds is going to advance a sale, you are out of your mind.

The "Rule of 7" states that people have to be touched by us at least 7 times before they begin to truly understand what we do and the benefits we can deliver. Most of the time, a "next step" in the sales process will not be a solid one if our prospect has not received multiple touches from us. Your system should recognize that reality and deliver those touches.

And, your system must be automatic. If you are customizing too much or you are dealing with prospects as individuals rather than as groups, the reality is that those touches will not be sent out by you. You will lose deals simply from a lack of organization.

Don't delude yourself into thoughts that you are going to create unique touches for each target. You won't do it and your system will break down.

Those who opt in to your Plan B are part of a group with similar needs and desires. Your goal is to make this group as large as possible and generate the most opportunities from this group as you can. The group will receive the same touch at the same time.

Those automatic touches must enable prospects to identify themselves to you when they are ready to move to the next step in the sales process.

We can probably agree that it is at least five times more likely that a sale will result if a prospect calls us rather than us having to chase them. Your system should encourage and make it easy for prospects to initiate action and contact you when they are ready.

20% to 25% of your meetings should result from prospects who initiated contact with you as a result of your automated system. This should occur after 90 days or so from the time you begin your automated system. After six months, 1/3 to 1/2 of your meetings should result from contact initiated by your prospects.

What do you think happens to closing ratios and the morale and motivation of your sales team when a substantial percentage of meetings are initiated by the prospects who are ready to buy?

That's right. And such a system is easier to set up and execute than you think.

In summary:

1. Your Plan B must contain an offer of information genuinely desired and helpful to your suspect.

2. Your Plan B must anticipate multiple touches.

3. Your Plan B system does not have you tracking touch dates for each individual target and putting something together specific for each target. Either:

   A. Targets will receive touches from you automatically without you having to remember or do anything, or

   B. Targets will receive touches as part of a group that receives the same thing at the same time. This makes it practical to get out the door.

4. Each touch must give targets multiple ways to "raise their hands" out of the crowd and identify themselves to you when they are ready to buy.

9
Plan B
Step By Step

*How to automatically get prospects to raise their
hand from the crowd when they are ready to buy*

Let's get the situation in focus.

You have called called and called and booked many appointments. By use of "potential worth" questions you have separated the targets with the highest potential from the low priority and no priority targets.

By use of effective responses to resistance, you have been able to go even further. You have booked meetings that would not otherwise have been scheduled, and from others you have obtained specific follow-up dates and the reason why it is important to call at that time. Your calls have given you good reconnaissance information as to future buying.

But what else can you do with a decision maker who gives you nothing, nada, zip?

Keep in mind that we are calling carefully selected target records, so we know with a high degree of probability that our targets, as a group, are likely to purchase what we have to offer.

Not only that, prior to getting a decision maker on the phone, we may have determined that they currently use what we offer, are likely to make a purchase in the future, or will be reviewing vendor relationships at some specific time.

What can you say to advance a relationship when your request for a meeting has been denied despite your best efforts. Your target may not know you well. Maybe you have no credibility in their eyes at this time. Particularly as to high potential targets, you must do something that will start to build a relationship and the perception of credibility.

What exactly do you do? Say *"Goodbye. Call you in six months?"*

No. You can do what I did initially and still do today.

Let me share two "Plan B" responses, then explain what makes them so effective."

Plan B response #1

"That's fine. Look... I do a lot of this and have a free email tutorial that includes many of the strategies that have proven effective. It's very popular and you probably would pick up at least a couple of good ideas. You can optout anytime. Can I put you on the list?"

Or,

"Mr./Mrs. top exec I don't want to be on your back but we do a lot of work in this area and companies like A, B and C have selected us for projects that worked well. I have put together a series of bulletins containing 23 specific strategies as to how you can _____ (fill in the benefit that is of interest to your audience) and we periodically send out E-mail tips on how you can _____ (fill in the benefit). Can I send them to you? Great. Your E-mail address is?.... Your mailing address is?....... And, when would be the best time for me to contact you again... ?

thankyouverymuchgoodbye. " Click.

Three times out of four the answer is "OK." Then comes the potential worth question if you do not already have the information. You now ask: ""*How many salespeople do you have?"* *"How many relocations do you do a year?"* (You know the drill.) The answer is obtained; goodbye's are said. Click.

What just happened? You didn't get a meeting. You did have a conversation with a top decision-maker at a company you believe would make a great client who gave you permission to communicate periodically.

That decision-maker is going to receive consistent communications from you calculated by their content and timing to drastically increase the odds that you can get an appointment – in six weeks.

THE ORIGINS OF THIS STRATEGY

In the course of my own business I had written a number of articles (a good number of which I thought were pretty darn good) and sent them out to those who had voluntarily opted into my E-mail blast list. People could optin by responding to my faxes, visiting my website or requesting it when seeing me at a seminar or training session.

Over time this list grew to be quite sizeable. Every couple of weeks or so I would write a new article and E-mail it to everyone. Every E-mail article contained an offer of information (typically a free CD of strategies). They could obtain this information by responding back to the E-mail or clicking a link that lead them to a landing page on my website where they could fill in a form to receive the information offer.

At that time much of my good business came from those who had first opted onto the E-mail list and then requested information at some time. I would send it out, follow-up and much business was developed.

The good news was that I had a marketing tool and process that quality prospects welcomed and responded to. It only cost me $20 a month. Heaven.

But.... I also had a problem. Those who opted into my E-mail newsletter didn't get the best articles that I had sent out previously. This was a major problem. The initial communications people receive from you go a long way to creating their perception of your value and worth. One touch every two weeks or so is not the optimum frequency to establish a good positive impression and, of course, you want all your new opt in's to receive your best material regardless of when they opt in.

The solution was sequenced E-mail. With this service, I was able to collect all the articles that I would want good new prospects to be exposed to and deliver them in a sequence and timetable I determined. No matter when a suspect opted into my list they would receive E-mail #1 immediately, then E-mail #2 three days later, then E-mail #3 three days after that, then E-mail #4 three days after that, on and on and on.

In addition to the sequence of E-mails they would also be on my blast E-mail list and receive all the new articles I sent out. A sample blast E-mail can be found at the end of this chapter.

The benefit of this was that those who opted in received the best impression possible from a series of E-mails delivered over about six weeks. They started to realize I might really have something that might benefit them. They responded back. They went to the website. They called me. Some even sent checks.

So I got to thinking.... what if I called this series of E-mails containing my best articles a "tutorial?" What if I started offering it to decision makers who turned down my initial request for an appointment?

I knew from experience that this series was well received. I was calling a very highly qualified target list. I decided to try it using a script like this.

After being rejected…

"That's fine. Look, I have a free E-mail tutorial on setting sales appointments, which has proven pretty popular. It contains many of the successful strategies and proven methods I have developed over the years. Can I put you on that list? I know you will pick up a few good ideas and you can opt out anytime."

About 75% of decision-makers spoken to, who did not agree to a meeting, would opt in to this "tutorial." I then did three things. 1) Write their E-mail address down. 2) At the end of my days calling, enter those E-mail addresses into my online sequenced E-mail autoresponder. 3) Enter a call back date into my contact manager which corresponded with the ending of the sequenced E-mail series (six weeks).

Nothing else need be done. These benefit-rich credibility messages, <u>which your target has given you permission to send to them</u>, go out on the schedule you set up without you having to do or remember anything. All for less than $20 a month.

You then call them back six weeks later at the end of the initial sequence.

The target now knows you… is fully informed of what value you can deliver… and has formed an impression as to your worth and credibility. The follow-up call is a very different conversation. It is a much warmer conversation than the initial cold call.

I have noticed two things. First, people are much more likely to take or return your calls. This makes sense since you are now perceived as a valued service provider (even an expert), not a dreaded vendor. Second, people open up to you about their needs and challenges. This is important since it enables you to properly code them and properly allocate your time and resources.

You may end up booking a meeting, or agreeing on a future action or deleting them from your list. All are important objectives.

Many times after you have established credibility, the good prospects call you because the E-mail info that you send makes it easy for them to do so by replying or filling out a simple form.

WHAT TO DO

To have something worthwhile to offer that will advance a sale when your target says "NO" or to get good quality prospects to "raise their hands" out of the crowd when you have been unable to reach them, you will need at least three things.

1. A sequenced autoresponder service.

2. An offer of information with a high perceived value that offers immediate benefits.

3. Consistent "touches" of information that remind your targets that you exist, that educate them as to what you do and that build credibility.

4. A website landing page that gives people reasons and the means to leave their contact information helps to build response and is a fourth tool you should consider.

The sequenced autoresponder is simple to set up, easy to use and cheap. If you send me the information update request form in this book I will send you the names of a couple of services I can recommend.

Essentially, what you do is create a series of E-mails that are full of stories, information, tips, strategies and just good stuff of interest to your targets. Then, you enter their E-mail address (you did get permission) and your target gets a sequence of high-value messages from you without your having to coordinate a thing.

Your targets hear from you consistently. They get information they value. They begin to understand your differentiation. They have an easy way to signal you that they need more contact or are ready to buy. And… it is all done without you doing a thing.

Not only that, but when your initial sequence of messages is complete you can also send periodic updates to the group very easily.

The articles you send must be carefully crafted to be beneficial to your targets while communicating what you do and building your differentiation in the marketplace. Likewise, these materials must build your credibility and make it easy for them to contact you when they have a need and are ready to buy.

My recommendation is that your initial series of touches be 12–15 messages long. It takes time to create awareness of the benefits you can provide and establish credibility. A few touches just won't do it. Remember also that it is unlikely your targets will read all of them. So if you create 12–15 you can be reasonably assured they will read at least half of them during a six week period.

Your touches need not be long. 600 words or so is fine. But don't get hung up on length. If it takes you longer to say what you need to say to communicate the message you wish, so be it. Although it is true that many targets will not read long messages, my experience is that a high percentage of the targets that buy will read them.

If someone doesn't have a need, they are unlikely to read a message of any length. If someone has a need and you are providing them genuinely helpful information, they will read a lengthy message, so don't be afraid to send out long E-mails.

GET THEM TO "RAISE THEIR HANDS"

In addition to sending them quality information, you must give those with more advanced needs the opportunity to identify themselves to you. You can do this by offering a "Special Report." But it doesn't have to be that. It could be a CD of you speaking on a topic of interest. It could be you interviewing an expert or author on a topic of interest to your targets (these people are amazingly easy to communicate with and I tell you how to go about it in the "Seminar In A Box" and distance learning classes).

I am personally partial to audio CD's. Not only are they simple and inexpensive to create but they establish credentials and credibility like few other marketing tools.

If you are an independent professional or consultant, if people are buying/relying on your company's knowledge or expertise, if you need to educate your audience about problems you can solve for them or benefits you can deliver (these may be problems they didn't know existed or benefits they had never thought of) audio CD's are a perfect tool.

Your prospect will listen to you for 30–45 minutes. They will hear your voice. They will form an impression as to whether you are smart or mediocre. They will be educated as to what you do and just how knowledgeable you are and what you might accomplish for them. This is a very rich form of communication. They are spending time with you up close and personal and you control everything they hear.

Your CD's are easy to create. They can be created for no money or less than $200. If you discount this strategy thinking you need to hire a studio or spend a lot of money, you are wrong. Many people I work with use this technique and create their own CD's with their home computer very easily. Many newer computers come with all the tools you need as standard equipment.

Larger companies tend to overcomplicate this strategy and make it a much larger cost and bigger production than it need be.

A 30 minute CD is about 14 pages double spaced. You can do that.

Another way to create your CD is to record a talk you give to a group. If you happen to speak to groups all you need is a portable digital recorder and you have your content. If you don't currently speak to groups, you could invite clients and prospects to a breakfast briefing where you will talk on some item of interest. This talk can be the content for your CD. If you don't have enough clients and prospects, invite your family and friends over. The CD will sound the same.

Even another option is for you to be interviewed by somebody and have that conversation recorded. You write down the questions you want your interviewer to ask and outline your answer to every question. You then sit down for a spontaneous interview. That conversation is edited for your CD.

Even if you don't use the CD option, that same content could be used in a special report or series of informational bulletins.

The bottom line is... that any information offer must build your credibility and provide multiple "touches" with your prospect. Remember the "Rule of 7". Our prospects have to be touched by us 7 times before they even start to realize we are communicating with them.

These communications should be automated (let's face it... you won't follow-up individually) and they have to be cost-effective... E-mail sequenced autoresponders are perfect tools.

Another option would be a series of postcards, letters or mini-newsletters, which serve the same purpose. Your targets hear from you consistently and begin to understand what you do as well as what your points of differentiation are and just how credible you are.

Your selection of which tool (or combination of tools) to use (E-mail, postcards, letters, faxes, newsletters or other options) has a lot to do with your desired cost per inquiry or cost per sale. This is a topic that goes beyond this book.

If you decide to mail your communications, my recommendation is that you send things out in groups. If you try to track each touch with each prospect, those touches will not get out the door. So what's the sense? Use your contact manager to code prospects and send touches out to the whole group.

HOW YOUR PLAN B STRATEGY CAN HELP YOU LIFT RESPONSE WHILE YOU ARE CALLING

When making your calls you need to obtain fax numbers. With each call cycle you leave a voicemail message and send a fax.

What does the most effective fax look like? First, a little background.

I first started using faxes about five years into doing appointment setting projects. The first project I used faxing was for a mid-sized consulting firm that was looking to meet with CEO/Presidents of companies with a minimum of $100 million in revenue in certain industries. Their goal was to obtain consulting projects worth $500,000 or more. Three faxes ultimately helped generate results on that project. One of those faxes can be found at the end of this chapter.

As you can see that fax is pretty straightforward. It was used with the idea that it could warm my suspect up prior to a conversation. Very few targets called back as a result of this fax, although a couple of very hot prospects did.

This fax was also used as a bridge with the executive assistant to the CEO/President. After I had exhausted my calling efforts and all efforts to get the target to pick up the phone had failed, I would use this fax as part of a "Hail Mary" strategy.

I would call the executive assistant to Mr./Ms./Mrs. Big and say *"This is Scott Channell from XYZ group. We are experts in _____. Corporations such 1, 2 and 3 have selected us. We have achieved results like _____. I was just calling to determine if Mr./Ms./Mrs. Big would like to review some strategies or options to accomplish _____. Can you help me?"*

The knee jerk response was always *"Let me take your name and number."*

To which I replied *"Well, why don't I send you a one page fax describing what we do and the results we produce. I'll call you back in a couple of days to see if Mr./Ms./Mrs. Big would like to meet or receive any information. That way I won't keep calling and be on your back."*

The relieved voice on the other end of the line (who now did not have to take a message) would reply "OK" and I would confirm the fax number and fax away.

A couple of days later I call the executive assistant back and get a yes, no or instructions to contact someone else in the organization. The fax allowed me to control the message that the top executive received. It worked pretty well. (By the way, when the CEO/President refers you to someone, you are almost guaranteed an appointment.)

Since that fax was working well and targets were responsive to my plan B offer of a tutorial and information offer, I decided to combine the two.

I designed a fax format that not only warmed up my targets, but enabled those who had advanced needs to identify themselves to me. They could opt in to an E-mail tutorial, request the information offer, they might visit the website and fill in the form there, or they might even call.

My thinking was that since I had an offer that had proven effective with my target audience, why not include it in faxes sent out as part of my initial setting sales appointments call sequence.

You can do the same.

1. Make a call to identify the decision maker, obtain the fax number and permission to fax.

2. Call the next day and seek to speak to the decision maker. If they don't pick up leave a voicemail and send a fax.

3. Three business days later repeat step #2.

4. Three business days later repeat step #2.

5. If during the course of your previous calls, you discover information that makes a target worth more time and attention, repeat this step additional times.

More worthwhile desired future accounts will identify themselves to you and you can follow up appropriately.

Your targets receive your fax with your powerful offer and some will enter your sales pipeline. I would recommend always offering your e-mail tutorial as an option in your fax because I find that many who wouldn't otherwise fill out a form will sign up for the tutorial. Maybe there is less commitment involved. I don't know. But, a good number of people enter your sales pipeline who would not otherwise be there when you use a fax.

The key to a good prospecting fax is an offer with high value as perceived through the eyes of your prospect.

This is powerful because your information offer does double duty for you. It gets decision makers who have declined to meet with you into your sales pipeline receiving benefit-rich credibility building messages they have requested. The same information offer boosts response during your call cycle even if you can't get your decision maker on the phone. You have provided alternate means for good prospects and potential future accounts to identify themselves to you.

Samples of faxes using this strategy can be found at the end of this chapter.

So, with a good "plan B" that requires virtually no additional effort and no additional costs of consequence, you dump more prospects into your sales funnel and greatly reduce your costs of inquiry.

IMPORTANT NOTICE ABOUT FAX USE

Some states, the F.C.C, and possibly other governmental agencies have enacted, proposed (or have under review,) rules that would limit the use of fax to certain business relationships and circumstances. These rules are evolving and may change significantly at any time. Before you use fax as part of your process, determine what the rules are currently that apply to you.

SAMPLE BLAST E-MAIL

Message header: Who is consistently setting sales appointments?

Truths?

Nobody important answers the phone.
You can't get by gatekeepers.
Voicemail is never answered.
Calling is boring.
No one agrees to meet with a stranger.
I would rather eat glass than prospect.

All "true" statements - almost all the time.

EXACTLY WHO IS CONSISTENTLY SETTING SALES AP-
POINTMENTS?
By Scott Channell
http://www.settingsalesappointments.com
http://www.scottchannell.com
Please refer to someone who may benefit.

But not... all the time. Those who are consistently successful
seem to fall into two distinct groups. There are lessons to be
learned here.

Group one: In startup or launch mode.
Group two: Very disciplined about their sales process.

If you are a startup or launching something new it is often... meet
and sell or die.

Clients in this category have included: 1) homebased business
gasping for air which set up 65 quality appointments within

months and quadrupled revenues, and 2) a mammoth energy utility that setup 200 sales appointments to launch a new division.

In both cases, these businesses were under extreme pressure to deliver revenue. More time was not an option. Meet and sell or die.

The second group is not responding to extreme short-term financial pressures and is very disciplined about their sales process. Clients in this category include a $100 million technology equipment supplier that improved their closing ratio 25% by setting more and better quality appointments, and the international relocation company that infused their sales pipeline with 500 new appointments in a year.

In the second category, these companies had sales discipline. They collected and studied their numbers and made changes accordingly.

Information and contact request form located below.

How many appointments to close a sale?
What is the average new account worth?
What does it cost to get an appointment?
What scripts work best?
What call process works best?

They know all this and more. They know their numbers. They do things to move their numbers.

The startups set sales appointments despite the "truths" listed at the top of this article because boredom and frustration pale next to financial ruin.

The disciplined group acknowledges and works within the "truths" to keep a steady stream of new revenue flowing. Their measuring systems, attention to process and desired financial results overcome the "truths."

Those in the middle, without a financial gun to their heads or sufficiently on top of sales process detail, let the "truths" be more powerful than their desire for improved sales results.

Where are you?

If you could use some help or guidance, return the form below or call me at 978-927-5099.

Best wishes with your prospecting,
Scott Channell
http://www.settingsalesappointments.com
http://www.scottchannell.com

SCOTT, PLEASE SEND THE FOLLOWING OR CALL ME.
Hit REPLY, fill in form, then SEND.

[   ] FREE CD of appointment setting strategies.
[   ] Send catalog and put me on mailing list.
    Details on speaking, training, coaching, products.
[   ] Call me to discuss my needs.

Name:
Title:
Company:
# of salespeople in company:
Address:
City State and Zip:
Phone:

Fax:
What I want to accomplish:

copyright 2004 Scott Channell

39 Dodge St. #288
Beverly MA 01915
978-927-5099
Fax 978-964-0199

NOTE THE MULTIPLE RESPONSE OPTIONS

Prospects can:
    1. Call.
    2. Reply to the E-mail.
    3. Go to a website where they can fill in a form to request contact or more information.

This works.

SAMPLE FAX #1

ONE MEDICAL CENTER WE ASSISTED FOUND DIRECT COST
REDUCTIONS TOTALING $1,765,000.00, IMPROVED
PRODUCTIVITY IN SOME DEPARTMENTS AS MUCH AS 30%,
AND INCREASED PATIENT COMMENDATIONS 80%.

December 23, 1996

WILLIAM BO███████

Dear :

Are your change efforts producing bottom line results
which are satisfactory to you?

If not, you might benefit from our experience with
hospitals. We can help you drive down expenses while enhancing
patient and physician satisfaction?

Our niche consultancy emphasizes behavioral change,
implementation and results. Our proven methods may help you to:

* Achieve sustainable improvements of
a meaningful nature.

* Identify the barriers to higher
productivity and customer satisfaction.

* Reduce rework, improve service and
increase throughput in departmental
core processes.

Health care providers and companies like AT&T,
Marriott, Eastman Chemical and Alcan, look to us for
implementation of *performance improvement strategies*
which are accelerated and measureable.

Would you like to obtain specific information on how
to obtain the above results?

Sincerely Yours,

Scott Channell
The ████████████
Direct 40██████████2

p.s. I'll call your office D.
If you will not be in, or this
is inconvenient, please have _____
tell me when to return the call.

SAMPLE FAX #2

TO: Daniel ██████
    Facility Manager
    CDM ██████████████   RE: Employee relocation strategies that save time,
                                  money and aggravation.

FROM: Carol ███████████   Would you like to review some tips and options
      ███████4 Direct   that have worked well for others?

Are you 100% satisfied with the service, responsiveness, reporting and cost-effectiveness of your employee relocation program?

If you would like some information, ideas and strategies that may improve the relocation process for you and your transferees— we would like to share some information with you.

Major corporations such as Raytheon Service Company, Talbot's, Polaroid Corporation, Duracell USA — and numerous smaller companies have chosen us to assist them with their relocation program. Let us share with you some of the strategies that have proven beneficial.

EMPLOYEE RELOCATIONS
12 Strategies To Save Time, Money and Aggravation.

Free Report

Every year companies entrust us with 1,600+ international relocations and thousands of domestic moves. You may benefit from service options and procedures chosen by many other corporations.

You have nothing to lose but headaches and excessive costs. Why not review this report and some other information.

If you would like to review some ideas and options which may assist you, check off your areas of interest below, correct contact information if necessary, then …

FAX TO 7██████████1

____ Send me your free report.
____ Call me to discuss improving our employee relocation program.
____ Send me information on your services. I am particularly interested in:
        ____ Drafting a corporate relocation policy ____ Outsourced relocation services
        ____ Domestic moves ____ International moves ____ Temporary housing

Please circle your annual move volume:

	under 10	11-50	51-100	101-250	251-500	501-1,000	1,000+
Domestic						25+	
International	1-5	6-10	11-15	6-20	21-15		

Faxed to 1-617-████████

██████████████████████████

Name/Title _____
Company _____   **INTERNATIONAL**
Address _____
City St Zip _____
Phone/Fax _____

SAMPLE FAX #3

Would access to top decision makers at desired accounts help you to sell more faster? What volume of new business would result if your sales team was consistently face-to-face with desired qualified prospects?
FREE TUTORIAL – FREE CD/AUDIOTAPE - PROVEN STRATEGIES
FAX THIS FORM OR START IMMEDIATELY AT WWW.FINDINGBUSINESS.COM

FROM: Scott Channell

Are you seeking some new options and strategies to cost-effectively generate qualified leads, set sales appointments with the real decision makers, qualify your opportunities, and shorten your sales process?

If you have the capacity to handle more new business, yet feel that a simple lack of the right information and guidance is holding you back — our experience and information may help you.

Qualified leads, worthwhile sales meetings and new profitable strategic sales don't appear by accident. We invite you to review some tips and strategies that have proven successful in a variety of industries.

Our typical client has a salesforce that is "too busy" or easily frustrated by prospecting efforts. Those obstacles can be overcome.

If you would like some options give me a call to discuss your situation or simply return this letter.

Best wishes with your sales efforts,
Scott Channell

WWW.FINDINGBUSINESS.COM

Scott Channell's
BREAKAWAY
G R O W T H   S T R A T E G I E S
Beverly MA Ph. 978-921-2018

Tips And Strategies To Set Sales Appointments With Top level Decision Makers.
FREE E-MAIL TUTORIAL
Winning scripts, overcoming stalls, voicemail strategies, handling gatekeepers.
Successful 30 second appointment setting scripts.
Organizing for prospecting success.
Opt-out anytime.

Enter E-mail address. Fax to **978-927-5500**

Want to set more sales appointments?

Get proven tips & Strategies.

FREE CD/AUDIOTAPE

_____ Send me CD/Audiotape.
_____ Send me info on your speaking, training and coaching options.
CALL 978-921-2018 OR FAX TO 978-927-5500

Name/Title _____
Company _____
Number of salespeople in company _____
Address _____
City St Zip _____
Phone/Fax _____

See notice as to fax use on page 135.

10

How To Set Up Your Prospecting System Step-By-Step

What to do and when to do it

Prospecting is not rocket science. The steps outlined below may seem like a lot to tackle, but if you look at each step individually, you will see that they are not particularly difficult. The power of this program lies in knowing all the steps and then executing them in a coordinated manner to get the result you seek at an acceptable cost.

1. DETERMINE YOUR ULTIMATE GOAL

This is not about setting appointments. This is about generating worthwhile, profitable sales at an acceptable cost. All efforts must contribute to reaching your pre-determined worthwhile goals.

Answer questions like this. What volume of new revenue do you seek? How many new accounts do you need? What is the average new account worth? How many sales appointments do you need to obtain one worthwhile account?

Answer those questions so that you don't end up setting appointments with prospects who don't buy or buy too little.

2. SELECT YOUR TARGETS

Sixty percent of your results come about merely by selecting the right targets. The most common mistake is made when someone is in a rush to jump start sales and starts engaging in activities to "see what happens." Big mistake.

Keep your eyes on your ultimate goals. You need accounts of a certain size that generate an acceptable profit margin. There are, of course, exceptions. But, almost always a large percentage of your best accounts will fit a certain profile. They may be in a certain industry, geographic area, or generating a certain sales volume, or have a specific range of employees.

Do not assume you know who your best targets are. Take a few short hours to list the current clients you have that you would like to clone in droves.

Add to that list your competitors' best clients that you would like to have. Now, next to each name on the list, write down specifically what you know or can find out about that company.

What is their specific industry SIC code... revenue range... workforce size... location... growth rate, etc. You may have to do some research to obtain this info, but if you know where to look it is quick and easy to get and invaluable to the success of your prospecting program.

Simply stated, 80% or more of your best prospects will fit into a standard profile. Spend too much time outside of that profile chasing the exceptions to the rule, and you will find yourself very frustrated and spending too much time and money to generate a qualified prospect.

When a soon-to-be-successful appointment setter contacts me and relates how their appointment setting efforts to date just have not worked out, the first question I ask is, "Who have you been calling?" The answer is almost always… a list we saw in the paper, some lists of top companies, the local Chamber of Commerce list (shoot me please) or some list recommended from a list company. No wonder their efforts were not successful.

If you get this step wrong… if you call a group of suspects that does not contain the most targets fitting your "best account" profile, no matter how good you are at all other steps of the appointment setting process, you are guaranteed to fail.

At the risk of boring you let me repeat… do not make the common mistake of saying to yourself, "I don't want to miss anyone," when selecting your list to call. That is dumb and self-destructive.

To be successful you must invest your limited time and resources where you can make the most progress toward achieving your goals. After you finish calling out your first group you get to call other groups of targets. So if there are other groups that you feel contain quality targets you can call them in subsequent rounds of calling.

Your initial group to call should include enough records for no more than your first three to six months of calling 1,000 to 2,500 records at most. No more.

You do yourself no favors if you buy lists in greater quantities trying to save two cents a record. The cost of your records to call is by far the smallest investment you will make. The value of the time you invest in working with those records is worth far more. Don't start purchasing in larger quantities until you know from experience that a group of records that fit a certain profile is the best group to call. Test small.

Example:

If you have profiled your best clients and found those specific records on publicly available database, and determined that 80% of your best accounts fall within SIC codes 8741, 8742 and 8748, tend to have a minimum of $2.5 million in revenue or at least 50 employees and are located in three digit zip code areas 014 – 024, 027 and 012, that is the group you should prospect first.

When you obtain a count of businesses fitting that profile with a list company, if you find there are at least 1,000 to 2,500 records that fit that profile, that is the list you should start with. If there are more, you should pick particular zip code areas to start with that will deliver the requisite number of records. My preference is to purchase all records that fit the "best account" profile in specific zip code areas rather than buy on a Nth name basis. That way, I know I have totally called out an area and when I buy more names from that list company the chances of duplication are small.

There is a publicly available database that enables you to look up specific company records and obtain their SIC codes, revenue ranges, employee ranges and zip code information for free.

If you send me the information request/update form found in this book, I will tell you where to find it. I will also send you my recommendation for the best source to buy complete and accurate lists of companies to call. I don't mention them here because I am concerned that things may change and the information in this book would not be up to date or accurate, thereby frustrating your appointment setting efforts.

3. SET UP YOUR PHYSICAL WORKSTATION

You need a basic computer with a printer and a fax machine nearby. In a perfect world you would have a headset and a direct phone line into your computer so that the computer will do your dialing for you. For software, you need a contact manager like ACT or GOLDMINE (each cost about $150), a fax program like WINFAX ($100 or less) and a simple desktop publishing program like MICROSOFT PUBLISHER ($100 or less) to create materials you will need. That's it.

4. SET UP YOUR CONTACT MANAGER FOR MAXIMUM EFFICIENCY

Let me be blunt. You must work with a contact manager that enables you to work very efficiently. If you are working with a paper system or are using a database that does not enable you to do all of the following, you are working with both hands and one leg tied behind your back.

Prospecting can be very boring and tedious work. If your system doesn't enable you to work at maximum efficiency and obtain the maximum number of appointments for your time investment, you will get frustrated and stop prospecting. This will cost you appointments, accounts, revenue, profits and commissions. Don't be defeated before you start. Work with the right type of contact manager and set it up correctly.

It is important that your contact manager enable you to do all of the following:

1. Slice and dice your suspect/prospect records. You must be able to segment and focus on sub-groups of records selected by any combination of the following criteria.

    A. Industry type/SIC code.

    B. Revenue range.

    C. Employee range.

    D. Active vs. inactive records.

    E. Inquirers vs. non-inquirers.

    F. Zip code location.

    G. The volume of the product/service you offer that they use or may use.

2. Add custom fields you must have. The fields you might add are:

    A. Refer to as.

    B. Business type.

    C. SIC code.

    D. Potential purchase volume.

    E. Rating

    F. Inquiry

    G. Employee range.

    H. Revenue range.

    I. Date of inquiry.

    J. Date of vendor review.

    K. Services/products fields.

3. Enable you to schedule a follow-up date for the next scheduled action.

4. Enable you to filter as a group all records scheduled for a call or follow-up activity on a particular date.

5. Enter important notes for a record.

6. Enable you to see at a glance everything that has previously occurred with a record.

7. Enable you to see at a glance everything that is scheduled to occur with a record in the future.

8. Allow you at the press of a key to print out letters, faxes and materials customized for a record.

9. Allow you to standardize repetitive notations.

If the contact manager you choose does not enable you to do all those things, you have just shot yourself in the foot before you begin a road race.

MORE ABOUT THOSE NECESSARY FUNCTIONS AND FIELDS

SIC codes:

All companies are categorized into Standard Industrial Classifications. All businesses are divided into divisions such as Agriculture, Mining, Construction, Manufacturing, Transportation, Wholesale Trade, Retail Trade, Finance, Insurance and Real Estate, Services and Public Administration.

All of those divisions are further divided into sub-divisions of two-digit SIC codes. For example, here are some of the sub-categories in the Services Division:

70 Hotels, Rooming Houses, Camps

71 Personal Services

72 Business services

73 Automotive Repair, Services & Parking

Those two digit sub-categories are further divided into 4-digit categories. For example, the *72 Business Services* sub-category is further divided into 4-digit categories, some of which are listed here for illustration.

7311 Advertising agencies

7335 Commercial photography

7349 Building cleaning services

7272 Prepackaged software

SIC codes are very useful in helping you to zero in on your very best targets. Know the SIC codes of your clients and best targets and have a field in your contact manager that contains the SIC code so that in the future if you wanted to focus just on "Commercial Photographers," or any worthwhile sub-group, you could do so.

Revenue range and employee range

Very simply you will have the opportunity to select records of targets of a certain size. If most of your business comes from companies with revenue in excess of $5 million annually it makes no sense for you to be calling companies that are smaller. If your best accounts are made up of mostly mom and pop's grossing less than $1 million annually, it makes no sense for you to be calling companies larger.

Revenue ranges are typically broken down as follows:

Less than $500,000

$500,000 to $1 million.

$1 million to $2.5 million

$2.5 million to $5 million, etc.

Employee ranges tend to be:

1-5

6-9

10-24

25–49, etc.

You want to know which of these ranges your best prospects fall into and have a field in your contact manager so that if you just wanted to focus on records that did $1 million or more in revenue or had at least 50 employees you could do so.

Active vs. Inactive records

Think of this for a moment. You call call call and at some point you are going to reach the point of diminishing returns for that record and stop calling. So you have a group of records you are actively calling and you have a group of records that contain perfectly good suspects whom you have called, decided to stop calling to focus on other records and have scheduled to follow up on at some specific time in the future (typically 4–6 months after your active call cycle ended). These are your inactive records.

How can you tell the difference between your active and inactive records? You code them.

I code active records as "3" and I code inactive records as "4." As soon as I identify a decision maker and begin a call sequence, I code that record a "3." When I reach the point of diminishing returns and I am going to give that record a rest for awhile so that I can go onto others I code it a "4." This way I can separate my active records from my inactive records.

Are there other codes that are helpful in your calling efforts? Yes, you are going to come across records that you don't want to call but don't want to delete either. There may be records that you are having difficulty identifying the decision maker on that you want to come back to at some time. There will be records that for some reason you feel deserve "special" or "priority" attention. Some records may be "red-hot" prospects. All of those categories can be coded.

Here is the coding system that has served me well in my "rating" field.

1. Worth little

2. On-deck

3. Active

4. Inactive

5. Special

6. Priority

7. Hot

By using this coding system I know which stage of the prospecting process all my targets fall into. When things get really busy and I can't follow up on everything I can be sure to at least follow up on my "special," "priority" and "hot" records.

Inquiries

When a contact makes an inquiry or schedules an appointment you want to place an "X" into your inquirers field. That way you can select all inquiries for special attention very easily.

Volume of product/services you offer that your target purchases or may purchase

If you are in the employee relocation business, it is important for you to know whether your target relocates 100 employees a year or 5 employees a year. In the sales training business it is important to know whether your target company has 200 salespeople or 2 salespeople. If you manufacture widgets, you want to know whether your target buys 5,000 annually or 5 million.

In the course of your calls you will be asking "potential worth" questions. This field, which you can label "worth" "volume" or whatever makes sense for your company, is where you put that information. Now if you want to spend more time and money on potentially larger volume users and less time and money on smaller volume users, you can do so.

Refer to as

This is a field I recommend you create and use to phonetically spell hard to pronounce names.

Date of vendor review

Many times you will learn that targets will be reviewing vendors on a certain date. If you create a field and make note of it, then you can implement a calculated plan to position yourself for the account.

Example: if you have 20 companies in this category for September, than 3 months prior to that you can implement a series of actions with that whole group, calculated to win you the business.

Services/Products fields

If what you offer contains a variety of products or services, consider creating fields that correspond to your major categories. That way, in the course of your calling and asking reconnaissance questions, if you discover that your target uses product x but not Y, you can approach them accordingly. When your group of identified product x users is large enough, you can select those records as a group and implement a strategy specifically targeted to their needs.

Standardizing repetitive notations

Standardize repetitive notations into simple codes and one keystroke. It makes no sense for you to write "called record, got voicemail, left message, sent a fax" 50 times a day. You'll shoot yourself. Standardize that into a simple result code that you can select with one keystroke. A decent contact manager will enable you to standardize these results so that you can make more calls and stay awake.

5. WRITE YOUR SCRIPTS

We have covered the format of a successful script previously. Here's a recap...you need three standard scripts.

You need an "Identify The Decision-Maker" script, a 30-second "Set The Appointment" script, and a "Voicemail" script. My recommendation is to type each of these double spaced on one sheet of paper that will be right in front of you when you call. Remember that the script you start with will not be the one you ultimately end up using.

As you call, you will make changes. It is not unusual to morph through 10-15 scripts before developing the one that flows off your tongue best.

6. CREATE YOUR SUPPORTING MATERIALS

You don't need a lot of support materials. But, what you do need is very important. You need a fax that you can use to supplement your calling so that those whom you cannot yet reach (but who may have an interest in your offer) can identify themselves to you. You also need some printed literature to send to those who request it... AND WHO YOU DEEM WORTHY OF RECEIVING IT.

Let's look first at the fax. The best prospecting faxes will restate the benefits of your offer, give prospects an incentive to identify themselves, have an obvious response device and provide specific instructions (for example: Fill out form below and fax to 978-927-xxxx). You can see some examples of winning faxes at the end of chapter 9.

Now, let's discuss your response to an information request. Responses should be in written, fax, or E-mail form and you should standardize these responses so that you can send them out with just a couple of keystrokes. If someone asks you to send something you want to be able to respond immediately. (Is this cutting edge or what?)

Don't be too quick to send information, though. Prospects shouldn't get information just because they ask for it. Being too agreeable to information requests is a fast road to appointment setting frustration.

7. DESIGN YOUR MEASUREMENT SYSTEM

You really only need three forms.

The first is a daily/weekly tracking form. On this form, you will track your key activities. Those activities typically are the number of meetings set, the number of conversations with decision-makers, and the number of new companies you initiate the process with. You will also want to keep track of how many companies are being actively pursued by you at any one time.

There is a certain rhythm to success. Over time, you may learn that in order to set x number of sales appointments, you must initiate your calling process with 50 newly identified decision makers a week. In order to set a sales appointment, you typically have to speak to six decision-makers and deliver your "set the appointment" script.

If you know your typical pattern and keep this info in front of you, you will have an early warning system when you start to deviate from your numbers. You can then take action to get back on track before it is too late.

Second, you need a weekly result sheet on which you track the specifics of your successes. When you set up a sales appointment, you would list out all the specifics of that appointment and any details known about the prospect. This is important because over time, you will notice certain patterns about the worthiness of certain appointments. With this kind of information, you will better allocate your time and target your efforts to those activities and records that tend to produce more worthwhile results for you.

Third, a conversation record. This is particularly important for new appointment setters. Every time you have a conversation with a decision maker make a brief note as to what happened. Did you set the appointment? Did you get the "send more info" blow-off? Very quickly you will start to notice patterns to your conversations. If you are getting a lot of "send more info" blow-offs and are not being successful at overcoming it, you will be able to identify that problem and change your strategy when you hear that response in the future.

Samples of these three forms can be found at the end of this chapter.

8. DESIGN YOUR INCENTIVE SYSTEM

Outside of carefully selecting your targets, I feel that a good incentive system for your teleprospectors is the most important reason that your program will consistently generate results at a reasonable cost. A big mistake that's often made is to set up an incentive system with goals that are unreachable. Management too often thinks that setting the goals high (before any extra money is earned) increases productivity. Nothing could be further from the truth.

Management should only be concerned with the cost per inquiry and the cost per sales appointment. You want to have a system where no matter what happened yesterday, or in the last two days, or during the last week, the appointment-setters can feel that if they do a good job that day, they can make more money. If you set a high monthly goal and the first week or so is poor, the appointment-setter mentally gives up for the month because the bonus goal is now out of reach. The same is true for a high weekly goal.

This is what works best. Assume that the average weekly productivity for a part time appointment-setter is six qualified appointments. The first small incentive payment should be earned at the 3rd or 4th meeting. An additional, increasingly larger payment should be earned for the 5th, 6th and 7th meetings each week. Because a bonus payment is always within reach, there is always the incentive to reach it.

I personally also like to see a small daily bonus. If a person has a great day, he/she can earn a small bonus sum for 2 or 3 meetings set in one day. What gets results is often counterintuitive. Small, incremental payments that are always within reach consistently generate leads and appointments at the lowest cost.

Incentive systems that set the bar too high destroy the motivation of the appointment-setter. Do not be concerned when your prospectors earn money. Be concerned only with your per inquiry or per appointment costs. That is what counts.

9. HIRING YOUR PROSPECTOR

These are difficult jobs to fill and retain. Turnover will kill an otherwise great program. Prospectors should be hired only for part time jobs. Let me repeat. These are part time jobs. Productivity decreases tremendously after 3 to 3 ½ hours of calling. You are fooling yourself to think otherwise. The best people are those who can earn more money with you than they could at their previous job and who value a convenient, flexible position.

There are a lot of smart, personable people making $10 an hour who think they are in heaven when they can earn $13 - $25 an hour with their incentive payments. There are also many people who value a flexible work situation. If you are willing to vary work hours and be flexible with working moms or mature adults, you can find loyal, hard-working employees who get results.

Here's a big tip. The most important interview is the first phone call someone makes to you inquiring about the position. Resumes are of little significance for these jobs. Evaluate their phone presence. That is what your prospects will be doing.

CONVERSATION RECORD

DATE _____ PROSPECTOR _____ CONVERSATION RECORD

	Company/Contact	Result	Worth	Notes
1				
2				
3				
4				
5				
6				
7				
8				
9				
10				
11				
12				
13				
14				
15				
16				
17				
18				

TRACKING SHEET

Week _____   Prospector _____   TRACKING SHEET

DAY	MONDAY	TUESDAY	WEDS	THURSDAY	FRIDAY	TOTAL WEEK
NEW DM'S IDENTIFIED						
CONVER-SATIONS						
APPTS SET						
OTHER						

New Dm's Identified   # of conversations   # appts set   Conversation to appt ratio

Weekly Totals _____ _____ _____ _____

Monthly Totals _____ _____ _____ _____

RESULT DETAIL

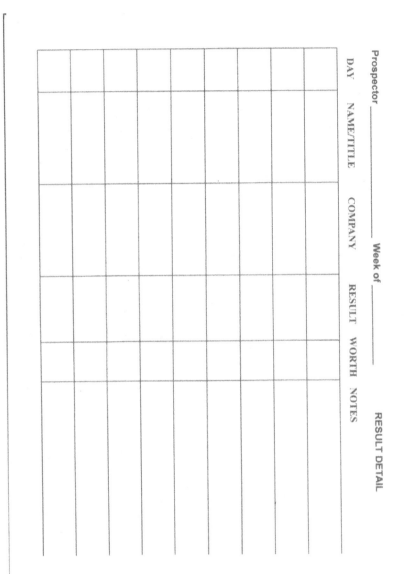

Prospector _____   Week of _____

RESULT DETAIL

| DAY | NAME/TITLE | COMPANY | RESULT | WORTH | NOTES |

11

Obtain New Project Fees With Four Prospecting Principles

Build a system that will be sustained

The most frustrating thing I see is people who start to get great appointments and fill their sales pipeline but then totally stop or prospect only erratically because they now need time to follow through on their great new opportunities.

There are four principles that come into play that enable you to have a sustainable prospecting system.

FLOW

This is the principle based on the fact that in any pool of suspects, there are only so many people who are reachable and who, once reached, would be receptive to your well-crafted, benefit-laden messages.

If there are typically 10 appointments in a group of 100 reasonably qualified targets, once you get them, you can call all you want but there are no more to be had in that group. No matter how many times you call, there are only so many people who will be receptive to your message in any group. So, to be successful, your system must "flow"... meaning that you are continually and systematically bringing new records into your process, working them systematically, then letting them go at some point.

The best way to determine that you have "flow" is to meet your goals for new decision makers identified and the number of records with which you launch your process every week. If you are doing that and completing your action steps with all your active records on a timely basis, that must mean that you are stopping at the point of diminishing returns. If you don't push them out the back end, you won't have the ability to bring more in the front end.

To have flow, however, you must be aware of the second concept...

YOUR POINT OF DIMINISHING RETURNS

You are in charge of your time. Not the people you call. Tire kickers don't waste your time... you do.

If (theoretically at least) there are 10 appointments in any group of 100, then as you book the 7th, 8th and 9th meetings, you should be thinking... *"Am I better off to continue calling the remaining 91 of this group to find that last meeting I'd expect... or should I call a new group of 100 that contains 10 meetings? What would be the best use of my time?"* You have only a limited specific amount of time to invest in appointment setting. You are the one who decides where to invest that time for the results you need. And, you must absolutely know when to let go.

In order to make that decision, you must have a consistent call process. That means that you have a consistent schedule or pattern of calls, voicemails, dials and faxes.

You will, of course, vary your call process in some instances. But, if you are varying too often, you don't have a call process. You have chaos and you are basing your financial future merely on wishes and good intentions.

If you continue to invest time and money with a group of people who make pleasant sounds, request information and ask that you call them back, yet never agree to meet — you are not in charge of your financial future. The tire kickers and time wasters are. You let them. It is your fault. Not theirs.

EFFICIENCY AND EFFECTIVENESS

Cold calling and prospecting is brutal work. It commonly defeats the strongest sales warriors. A sudden tsunami of activity (although temporarily powerful) will never generate the consistency you need to build and sustain a profitable business. To do that, your prospecting process must be efficient and effective.

A process that reliably has you speaking to four prospects an hour is more efficient than a process that has you speaking to only one prospect an hour. A process that enables you to dial the phone 40 times an hour is more efficient than a process that has you making 15 dials an hour.

Without efficiency, you get fewer chances to be effective.

Effectiveness is the measure of your success in converting conversations with targets to the result you seek. A good conversion rate may be one appointment for every 5 conversations. Increase your conversion rate by delivering a calculated, concise, benefit-laden message. If your conversion rate is too low, test alternative pitches and voice deliveries.

Know where the problem lies. Maybe you are very effective if you get someone on the phone but you just don't speak to enough people. Focus on increasing your efficiency for results.

Conversely, you may speak to a lot of targets who are not receptive to you. Focus, then, on increasing effectiveness for better results.

MEASURE RESULTS, NOT ACTIVITY

You tend to get what you measure.

I recommend that you measure only three things. In order to sell a big-ticket item, you typically need a face-to-face meeting with a real decision-maker. To get a meeting, you will usually need to have a conversation with that person. The most reliable indicator of future conversations is the number of new suspects with whom you initiate your call process on a daily or weekly basis.

So, I only measure three things. Meetings, conversations, new decision-makers identified. That's it. I don't measure "dials" because the number of dials is not rationally related to results.

You get what you measure. Measure results only.

12

Getting More Sales Appointments Without Improving Your Other Skills Guarantees Nothing

This is really about closing sales. Setting appointments is only one step of the process

You need to learn:

- How to avoid a flood of new appointments that produce no sales.

- Two reasons why the meetings you initiate require new tactics.

- Five things you must establish to have even a chance at collecting a check.

Setting more sales appointments is a necessary first step to new account generation. Yet, sales and revenue increases may not materialize without taking a critical look at your sales process.

When you substantially increase your rate of access to targeted companies, your expectations and sales approach must adjust to avoid serious disappointment.

Enhancing "first meeting" skills and increasing focus and attention on making advancements in the initial stages of the sales funnel are necessary to realize your revenue expectations.

If your mindset is, "We know how to close. All we have to do is get in front of more decision–makers to meet our goals" .... you are usually deluding yourself and headed for disappointment.

Example #1

A 40-person company currently closes 50% of accounts they gain access to. Typical sales are in the $75,000 — $175,000 range. The most desired sales are in the $300,000 — $600,000 range. Inquiries are generated from speaking and article publishing by key personnel.

This company seeks more access to decision-makers at targeted companies, which could result in those $300,000 - $600,000 sales.

In this first example, the sales team is used to seeing people who know them by reputation. Prospects have heard a top officer speak or read a published article. (Speaking and publishing, by the way, are the two best marketing methods for communicating credibility.)

So, when people call this sales team they have a recognized need and believe that this company can help them.

But but but... when salespeople initiate sales appointments, the meetings will be with people who don't have the same frame of reference. They may not know the company at all. They also, typically, will not be fully aware of all the benefits they could get from use of their service.

It is wrong to assume a high close rate in these circumstances.

The solution is below.

Example #2

A current coaching client of mine has recently realized a quick flurry of new appointments with targeted companies. The good news is that all of those companies would be great accounts. The danger is that without sharpening "First Meeting" skills and implementing some new contact and credibility strategies in the beginning stages of the relationship — my coaching client will fail to make the advances necessary to be at the table when a new vendor is selected by all those companies.

Why is this?

When you drastically increase the number of first appointments, it is possible that: 1) Prospects actually know very little – if anything at all – about you; 2) that they are in the very early stages of the buying process; or 3) that they have no present intent of buying. The meeting serves an introductory and information purpose only.

You must approach the meetings you choose to accept with a heightened awareness of what is necessary to earn an advancement. You have much to accomplish in 30 to 60 minutes.

Gaining access is only one step to gaining a foothold in an account with potential. Your ability to "manage the mix" and "earn advancements" will be as critical to meeting your sales goals as initially gaining access is.

MANAGING THE MIX

You must properly "manage the mix" of new appointments.

If you go on too many short sales cycle, small-volume meetings, accounts and margins will suffer.

If you go on too many long sales cycle, large-volume account appointments, not many will close in the short run. That kills your cash flow.

If you go on too many appointments and don't have the time or support to follow up, you are doomed to failure because your new contacts will not receive the frequency or quality of communication necessary for them to feel comfortable writing you big checks.

EARNING ADVANCEMENTS

Nobody does business with anybody that they don't trust and respect. When you start to secure sales appointments, many of the people you see will have little knowledge of your company or the benefits you offer.

Before you even have a fair shot at selling anything, you have to establish trust, respect, credibility and comfort while you effectively communicate value.

More frequent communication is better than less frequent communication. A consistent message is more powerful than an inconsistent message. Clarity and conciseness when communicating value has more impact than spraying and praying.

THE BOTTOM LINE

Setting sales appointments alone is no guarantee that you will reach your sales goals. More sales appointments, however, will force you to evaluate your skills and strategies in making advancements and managing your time.

You will change and adapt or you will leave a lot of money on the table.

13

Your Prospecting Strategies Should Increase The Size Of Your Average Sale

Don't just seek more. Seek more of the best.

How can prospecting strategies help you to increase the size of your average sale?

To accomplish this two things need to be done.

1. Refocus targets selected and the list used.

As a generalization, targets often have common characteristics. Typically, they may be in specific industries and have a certain range of sales volume or number of employees that make them more likely as a class to buy more.

Typical problem. A salesperson contacted me as they had purchased a database on CD. This was a problem for him because those tools usually don't provide acceptable levels of segmentation so that you know (with a high degree of certainty) that everybody you call has a high probability of buying more.

Here's my advice. Invest a relatively small amount of money in a quality list that you can have unlimited use of and be able to download right into your database. Such a list should include only records that meet all your specific selection criteria. If the list you start with is of all manufacturers, rather than manufacturers with sales volume in excess of $5 million annually, you are pretty much doomed before you even start. Do not put yourself in the position of wading through too many low probability low sale no sale suspects to save a few dollars. Your time calling those records is worth much more.

Tip. Make sure that those segmentation criteria you use are properly coded in your database so that you can slice and dice your list to maximum advantage.

2. Alter the scripting used to set appointments and "qualify."

Keep this in mind. Some people lie. Some people don't know. Some people won't tell you. So, if you are going to ask questions over the phone and expect to get straight answers, you are naive. But we do know this. A group of people who tell you they have a need and would be comfortable spending $xxxx on a project are a better class of prospects than those who don't.

So, after you have used your winning "Set The Appointment" script (modeled, of course, on previous lessons) you should ask two additional questions that qualify prospects for money and timing.

1. *"Mr. Prospect, our average project is in the $5,000 to $7,500 range. Is this the range you have budgeted for this project?"*

Since our goal is to weed out the smaller projects, this question is non-threatening and provides insight into the odds of a prospect's investing $5,000 or more.

2. *"Mr. Prospect, if our price were right and you felt comfortable with everything, what would you do?"*

If they say: "Hire you to start in one month" that's a great appointment. If they start talking about speaking to someone else, convening a committee, checking with the finance person for budget authorization, etc... then bells and whistles should start to go off in your head and you should probe deeper before deciding what you should invest with that prospect at that time.

14

Seven Sales Productivity Mistakes To Avoid

Don't duplicate these failure traps

MISTAKE #1. The belief that the "right information" will make a difference.

Not having the right information is rarely the biggest obstacle to improving sales results. Telling people the right things to do rarely gets results.

Insights from selling masters are available easily and cheaply in books and tapes. We have all attended presentations that are full of great ideas. Yet, in spite of soaking in all this great information, all too little seems to change for most of us.

New ideas are never going to help the people who are only using half of what they already know and only doing half of what they know they should be doing.

MISTAKE #2. Preparation is not the same as action.

If five people are on a cliff and three decide to jump, how many are left? Answer? Five. Why? Because deciding to jump and actually jumping are two different things!

So it is with sales training. You can be determined to increase sales or improve margins or both. You can acknowledge that improving your sales results will mean altering work habits, organization methods and your sales process.

You can also enthusiastically announce to the world your determination to increase results. But, actually changing is quite another story.

It's like paying for your gym membership every month yet not going. You feel better as you convince yourself that you have taken a meaningful step toward fitness. The reality is that all you have done is waste resources while months pass by.

MISTAKE #3. Seeking a large solution rather than a series of consistently larger successes.

The more ambitious the training goal, the longer it takes before you can start to implement anything. There is just too much to absorb. As time dribbles on, priorities change; people come and go; and the competitive marketplace further evolves. These factors make your training less relevant.

MISTAKE #4. Not having good communication between the sales coach and the organization.

If there is not effective communication between coach and corporation, the odds are that the information will be too complex or too far outside an organization's comfort zone to expect people to implement anything of substance.

Worthwhile training is a collaborative effort. There is always more than one way to achieve a desired result. There should be serious discussion of the pro's and con's of all options.

MISTAKE #5. Wanting results superior to others but doing that which is common and generally accepted.

Hello! If you want to do what everyone else in your industry is doing, yet get vastly different results, you need a reality check. If you decide to use the same marketing tools and sales methods and interact with your suspects and prospects very much like your competition. . . why would you expect superior sales results?

Mistake #6. Defining success as the delivery of information rather than as a measurable sales result.

Obtaining the right information and answers is not success. Success can only be obtained after initiating change that contributes to reaching a predetermined worthwhile sales goal. Quality information and answers can only support that change process. It is not success in its own right.

MISTAKE #7. Being too quick to accept a sales consultant's pre-packaged solution.

You may have a sales problem and a sales consultant may have a solution. But when the applause dies down, how likely is it that the program will contribute to initiating change and increasing sales productivity?

Before any program is delivered, there has to be frank and honest discussion about: sales goals, when results can reasonably be expected, the time and resources available and the organization's willingness to implement/support changes in strategy or work habits.

Brilliant ideas about what ought to be done come easily compared to the actual ability to make needed changes happen. Let's state the obvious. If you need to improve sales results, it's not going to happen if you do (essentially) what you always have done before.

If you or your organization is unable (or unwilling) to make and support the types of change recommended by a training program. . . why bother at all? Find this out before you invest a lot of time and money.

Have a discussion with any sales consultant about how much his/her recommendations and suggestions will vary from your current practices. If the reality is that they will take too much time, or cost too much money or simply will not be accepted / adopted by the sales force, don't proceed.

Are you just "too busy" to focus on worthwhile strategic thinking? Do you tend to make impulsive decisions about new strategies just to "see what happens?" Are you always disappointed about results (have unrealistic expectations)? Do you too easily excuse those who continue with work habits that fall short of goals? Well, if too many of these things apply to you and you don't alter those behaviors, no sales training program in the world will help you.

15

A Day
In The
Life Of An
Appointment Setter

What to do step-by-step

What does a typical day look like in the life of a successful appointment setter?

This chapter assumes that you have spent the few hours necessary to make sure that you can work efficiently (have a high number of conversations with top-level decision makers daily) and effectively (convert a reasonable number of those conversations to appointments or, failing that, gaining permission to launch your "Plan B" strategy).

This means that you have spent just a few hours profiling your best clients, specific great accounts you would like to have and your competitors' best clients. From that profile you have learned the characteristics of your best suspects. You know their SIC codes, revenue and employee ranges and geographic location. Using that information you obtained a list of ONLY THOSE TARGET ACCOUNTS.

You took this list and imported it into your contact manager (the most popular are Goldmine and ACT). You were careful to invest about an hour to create customized fields to import information critical to your ability to focus on records that will generate the highest payback for the time invested. Chapter 10 gave you the specific instructions to follow.

You also have the templates necessary for you to create customized necessary prospect communications with a few keystrokes. You also have your tracking data to review.

You have posted your winning scripts, responses to resistance, list of names to drop and results you might refer to right in front of you so that your conversations will be powerful, compact and full of benefits.

You are ready to smile and dial.

1. ASK YOURSELF SOME QUESTIONS

Where am I in relation to where I need to be? You have previously analyzed your close rate and average new account value so you know how many new first appointments you have to schedule with prospects that fit a certain profile to have any chance of meeting your sales goals.

Let's assume you are on track.

When you look back upon your work for the last six weeks or so you will see that you have hit your targets for new decision-makers identified you have launched your call process with, have had sufficient conversations with targets to have a chance at setting the number of appointments you need, and converted a reasonable number of these conversations to appointments. Congratulations.

But if you are not on track, you have to fix the right problem. It is rare that everything is broken. It is probable that only one or two components of your appointment setting system need fixing, but which ones? This is a stupid analogy but it fits. I got through school working construction and laying pipe. We used to say that a pipe was only as good as its weakest point. Lay a mile of pipe expertly and one small crack makes it worth little. Find and fix that one crack and everything works great. If your appointment setting system isn't working, look for the cracks to fix. Don't think everything is broken.

In order of probability, if you are not hitting your goals it is probably for one of these reasons.

A. You are calling the wrong targets. If you did not spend a few hours profiling your clients and best future accounts and select records to call based upon specific SIC codes, revenue and employee ranges and geography, stop and do that now.

If you get this step wrong, it matters little what else you do right. You won't set appointments, or if you do, they will be with the wrong targets and you won't sell much.

B. You are not hitting your daily/weekly targets for new decision-makers identified with which you launch your calling process. If you are not doing this you don't even have a chance of talking with enough new people to meet your sales goals. If you are making calls, you are talking to the same pool of targets over and over and getting nowhere. Surprise!

C. You are not having enough conversations with decision-makers. Focus on strategies that will increase the number of conversations you have with targets.

D. You are not converting enough conversation with targets to appointments. What is the real issue? If very few are agreeable to your initial "set the appointment" script, work on that. If people are agreeing to your initial script but you are having difficulty scheduling an appointment when responding to resistance, work on your response to specific forms of resistance.

My recommendation is that you work on these issues in order. Get good at a particular step before you move on to master the next one. Be conscious about improving at all times but focus on one step to master before moving on to another.

Having analyzed where you are in relation to where you should be and now that you know where you have to improve, you are ready to call.

2. IDENTIFY DECISION-MAKERS

In order to set appointments we must be constantly talking to new people. There are only so many people who are reachable and who will agree to meet with you. You should know your ratio of first meetings to a new account. You should know how many records you must call to get an appointment.

Usually you will get one appointment for about every 10 records called. If you need 5 appointments a week to meet your sales goals you <u>must</u> identify 50 new decision-makers a week (10 a day) to have a chance of meeting your sales goals. Identify less and you have no chance of meeting your sales goals.

You start by activating a filter in your contact manager that contains your uncalled records. You start with the first one, dial, and use your "identify the decision-maker" script on the receptionist. You obtain the name and fax number and, if possible, potential worth information. You add this info into the appropriate field in your contact manager, code this record a "3" in the appropriate field (designating it as a record you are actively working) and schedule a call for the next day.

You repeat this process until you identify your 10 new suspects with whom you will launch your call process.

My experience is that you can identify 12 new decision-makers an hour. I wish it was more but it isn't. Therefore, you have to allocate about an hour a day to complete this step in the appointment setting process. If you are identifying fewer than 12 per hour you are probably making a couple of classic mistakes. You are either surfing the internet for information on the company (a tremendous waste of time at this stage) or scrolling through your records trying to decide whom to call. Don't make either mistake.

You must think in terms of groups. You have only so much time and you must launch your call process with a requisite number of qualified records to have any chance of meeting your goals. You must also follow-up and complete all your scheduled calls. If it takes you two hours to complete this step when it should take you one, you will fail because you are misallocating your time.

If you are not identifying about 12 decision-makers an hour, be tough on yourself in evaluating the reason why. Then fix it.

3. COMPLETE SCHEDULED ACTIVITIES FOR THE DAY

You never complete an action without scheduling the next activity on that record. Never. If you don't, you will waste countless hours scrolling through your records to see if there is someone you should be calling.

Call up your filter for all calls or actions that have to be made that day. If you see "stragglers," activities scheduled for previous days that have not been completed, make every effort to complete them. If you often have many stragglers, it means you are not making your calls on schedule and your results will suffer.

Work from the list and call each one without getting distracted. Your goal should be to complete these calls within a certain time period. Stay focused.

When your decision-makers pick up the phone, slay them with your "set the appointment" pitch and respond to resistance effectively.

If you don't get an appointment or call back date acceptable to you, go right into "plan B." Schedule a next action on that record.

If your decision-maker doesn't pick up the phone, leave your voicemail script and send your personalized fax. Schedule a next action on that record.

Most of the time a 3 cycle touch system works best. Leave 3 voicemails and send 3 faxes roughly 3 business days apart before determining you have reached the point of diminishing returns and moving on. If you determine that you have reached the point of diminishing returns, code the record a "4" in the appropriate field (designating it as an inactive record – a perfectly good record with decision-maker identified that is not currently being actively called) and schedule a next action date for between four and six months away. You will then start the cycle all over again.

As to most of your dials, you will not speak to your decision-maker. You should try to obtain two bits of information that will greatly increase the number of future conversations and assist you in properly allocating your time between higher value and lower value suspects.

You want to make every effort to obtain the direct dial or extension number and get some indication of the potential worth of the account.

First, as to the direct dial or extension number: dial back the receptionist and in the most bored nonchalant non-caring voice you can muster, say something like this. *"Hi, I just called Mrs. Big and got the voicemail. I was just looking to send a package over anyway. Just so I know what to send, do you happen to know about how many salespeople there are in the company now?"*

This is the potential worth question? You find out here as to many records whether they are high value or small value. What is your potential worth question. What tidbit of information gives you some clue as to how much your business volume you might do with this suspect?

Once they respond, you then say *"Great. For when I call in the future, do you happen to know the extension number?"* You will be surprised how many times you get it.

I have found that people are much more willing to give you information that they don't think you really want. So couch what you really want as an afterthought and you will get it more times than if you asked for it directly.

Here is another "get the direct dial number strategy." Purposely call a wrong department. When the puzzled voice says, *"He/she doesn't work here. You want finance."* You can say *"Oh, I'm sorry. Could you transfer me?"* While they are looking up the number ask, *"Do you happen to have that extension for the next time I call?"*

As to every record you dial: make an effort to improve the quality of the information you are working with. Confirm the decision-maker, spell check the name, get the title, get the direct dial, get some indication of worth.

Remember that all records are not created equal. One of the reasons why you collect potential worth information is so that you can spend more time with the more valuable suspect accounts.

So let's assume you have made your first pass through all records scheduled for an action that day. One of the things that I used to do was to leave a voicemail for the smaller value records and schedule my next call for three business days later. Those smaller value records got just one dial. As to those records that had more value, when I heard the voicemail I would just hang up and not leave a message.

Later in the day I would call these remaining records again and go through the same drill. If they picked up the phone, I attempted to book the meeting. If they didn't, I would hang-up when I heard voicemail. I would repeat this one more time at the end of the day.

So what was I doing here. I was spending more time with higher value records. Making more dials to higher value records than I was to smaller value records. This led to more conversations with higher value suspects and subsequently more appointments set with higher value suspects.

What positions you to properly allocate your time is asking the potential worth questions.

What greatly increases the number of conversations you have with a more valuable segment of your suspect pool? You have asked the questions to obtain that information then purposely allocated more time to that group.

3. HOW TO SQUEEZE OUT ANOTHER MEETING OR TWO

All right. As to all your foundation steps you are on top of your game. You are identifying decision-makers and completing activity steps within the time you have allocated for them. You have scripts and responses to resistance that are working. You want more.

Here is how to get it.

Power calling.

By asking all those potential worth questions, and obtaining those direct dial numbers and coding records "active" or "inactive" you have positioned yourself for a major productivity payback.

Let's recap. You have dumped 10 new decision-makers a day into your appointment setting process. So after a month you have a pool of 200 and in five short months a pool of over 1,000 suspects highly qualified with decision-makers identified and potential value noted.

The single biggest factor that will increase the number of appointments you set will be the number of conversations you have with those you target. You increase your access to the suspects with the highest potential business value by first identifying them, allocating more time to them, and directing more dials to them.

Set your filter for all active records. Dial the first record.

Got voicemail? Hang up. No message.

Not in? In a meeting? Say, "Thank you, no message." Click. Do not identify yourself.

You can make 60 or more power call dials in an hour when your system is set up properly (contact manager that filters and delivers the next record to you quickly and automatically dials the phone).

Want to be even more focused? Set your filter to deliver only active records with a potential value over X or more. Set your filter to deliver only records with which you have the direct dial or extension number (my favorite).

Your inactive records can also be a great source of a couple of appointments every week you would not otherwise have scheduled. Remember, your "4's" (inactives) are suspect companies that fit your best target profile with which you have identified a decision-maker but just were not able to get them on the phone. You may have reached the point of diminishing returns as far as investing the time to leave voicemails and send faxes, but if they picked up the phone that would be a conversation you would want to have.

So, set your filter to deliver only your inactives, or include your inactives in your power calling when you find yourself in a situation where you need more conversations to meet your appointment setting goals.

By dialing in rapid succession without leaving messages or dealing with gatekeepers, you increase the number of conversations you have. That is the most important factor in how many appointments you set.

4. FINAL THOUGHTS

A. Beware of thinking "it's a numbers game" or measuring dial activity. The prospecting graveyard is overflowing with people who set all sorts of records for activity and dials and were unsuccessful at scheduling appointments. If you measure activity (dials) that is what you tend to get. Measure results (decision-makers identified, conversations and meetings set) and that is what you tend to get.

B. There are no bad times to call. There are those who swear that you can't call first thing in the morning, on Friday afternoon, during the lunch hour, at the end of the day, etc., etc., etc. They are delusional. Just call. The only time period I have noticed that appointment setting productivity falls off the map is the period between Christmas and New Year's.

C. Call after hours for 3 hours and 45 minutes per week. Three times a week call 1 1/4 hours just before the office opens up or closes. You already have your decision-makers identified and many times you have the direct dial or extension numbers. You will have conversations and set appointments with people you would not otherwise reach during the day.

Utilize time zones to your benefit. When I called from the Boston area I could spend 4 hours calling people between 7:45 AM and 9:00 AM. Using the power calling strategy you will have many additional conversations and schedule many more additional appointments.

Best wishes with your prospecting,
Scott Channell

Four Contrarian Truths About Appointment Setting

#1: The results you obtain in any given week has more to do with what you did two or three week prior, than it has to do with the quality and quantity of your effort during that week.

What you say, Scott? I made this point in a training session recently to be greeted with absolute silence — until the most successful appointment setter in the group spoke up to say that she also found this to be very true. As a result of this truth, she always made a point of identifying a certain number of new decision makers to be dumped into her appointment setting funnel every day and every week.

To appreciate this contrarian truth you need to accept three concepts. First, that there are only so many targets within any reasonably qualified group of suspects that are reachable and who would agree to meet with you. Second, that there is a combination of actions implemented (dials, conversations, faxes, voicemails, responses to resistance, etc.) within a defined period of time that is most calculated to get you the result you seek. Third, at some point we reach the point of diminishing returns with a record and need to set it aside for awhile to give you the time to prospect a new record.

If you accept that there are only so many in a target group that would agree to meet, then when you stop dumping fresh new suspects which contain records that are reachable and would agree to meet with you into your prospecting funnel, you end up dialing over and over again to the rest of the group - the part that contains those who are unreachable and who won't agree to meet.

So, if during any week or two you don't dump new records into your funnel, as you work your pre-defined best prospecting process on your records, you end up dialing well beyond the point of diminishing returns and seeing your results plummet.

#2: The more knowledgeable and helpful you are, the less likely it is that people will agree to meet with you.

Hmmmmmmmmmmmm. Let's see. We want high level people to be impressed with the extent of our knowledge and abilities and believe that we can help them, but if we actually demonstrate the full extent of our knowledge and abilities and try to help them, the odds of them meeting with us actually decreases?

That's right. You've got it now.

You see, people fully expect to turn down your request for a meeting. There is a knee-jerk powerful gravitational force working within suspects that is propelling them to conclude, "It's not worth my time to meet." When you maintain the curiosity factor and/or the promise that information they seek can only be delivered at a face-to-face meeting, then your suspect can conclude that the trade of their time for the information they will obtain at that meeting is a reasonable exchange for them.

If you go too deep, answer too many questions, succumb to your desire to immediately demonstrate just how knowledgeable and helpful you are, now your suspect is not so curious anymore and has received the information that is most important, so the exchange of time for information equation doesn't look so beneficial anymore. Also, without obtaining specifics from the potential client it is very easy to make assumptions over the phone which don't apply and have the suspect conclude — that's not me, so it's not worth my time to meet.

What you leave unsaid is more powerful that what you say.

#3. The best way to sell more of your product or service is to make every effort not to sell your product or service during the set the appointment phone call.

Say what? Don't try to sell what I am trying to sell?

Absolutely! You are one very intelligent appointment setter.

Selling an appointment that would enable you to sell your product or service is very different from actually selling your product or service. In the same way that you don't conduct a first meeting with a prospect like you do the 2nd or 3rd meeting (as they are distinct and separate steps in the sales process requiring the use of different strategies and emphasis) the set the appointment call is a distinct step requiring unique strategies and emphasis.

Don't mix steps. Don't skip steps. Stay focused on selling the appointment and you will get many more opportunities to sell your product or service to qualified prospects. Try to sell your product or service too early and you will meet with far fewer qualified prospects.

#4. Successful appointment setters make fewer dials.

You can rank "make more dials and you will set more appointments" right up there with "work harder and you'll make more money." Both are absolutely false.

Assuming that you are making a reasonable number of dials, the actual number of dials you make is not one of the most important factors in appointment setting success. The most successful actually make the fewest dials. The calls they do make result in more conversations, and the conversations they have convert to more appointments. Those are the real issues.

Making more dials with a flawed process will lead you only to frustration land. Focusing on the real issues -- having more conversations with qualified suspects and converting more of them to appointments, will get you more great opportunities to sell.

Best wishes with your prospecting,
Scott Channell
www.settingsalesappointments.com
www.scottchannell.com

FREE AUDIO CD OF STRATEGIES
AND UPDATE REQUEST FORM

If you would like:

1. Recommended autoresponder services.
2. Full size versions of the sample faxes for easier reading.
3. What publicly available databases you can reference to determine SIC codes, revenue and employee ranges, zip codes and more.
4. Full size versions of the tracking forms.
5. FREE AUDIO CD of additional strategies and other updates from date of publication that may help you.

Simply fax or mail this form to me or make a request online. If you need help or have a question I will contact you.

SCOTT, send me the audio CD of strategies and information above FREE. I also could use help with the following:

_____

_____

_____

_____

Name

_____

Company

_____

Address

_____

City St Zip

_____

Email

_____

# of salespeople in company

_____

Phone/Fax

_____

MAIL TO:

Scott Channell
Finding Business
39 Dodge St. #288
Beverly MA 01915

FAX TO:

978-964-0199

ONLINE:

settingsalesappointments.com/
prospectingupdate.htm